Collins gem

KU-157-215

GREEK
PHRASEBOOK
& DICTIONARY

Published by Collins
An imprint of HarperCollins Publishers
Westerhill Road
Bishopbriggs
Glasgow G64 2QT

Fourth Edition 2016

10 9 8 7 6 5 4 3 2 1

ISBN 978-0-00-813589-8

Collins® and Collins Gem® are
registered trademarks of HarperCollins
Publishers Limited

www.collinsdictionary.com

Typeset by Davidson Publishing
Solutions, Glasgow

Printed and bound in China by
RR Donnelley APS

If you would like to comment on any
aspect of this book, please contact us at
the given address or online.

E-mail: dictionaries@harpercollins.co.uk

 facebook.com/collinsdictionary

 @collinsdict

Acknowledgements
We would like to thank those authors
and publishers who kindly gave
permission for copyright material to be
used in the Collins Corpus. We would
also like to thank Times Newspapers Ltd
for providing valuable data.

Editor
Holly Tarbet

Contributors
Mary Cole
Panayota Koliatsa
David White

For the Publisher
Gerry Breslin
Janice McNeillie
Helen Newstead

Front cover image: National Library of
Greece in Athens.
©Anastasios71 / Shutterstock.com

Using your phrasebook

Whether you're on holiday or on business, your **Collins Gem Phrasebook and Dictionary** is designed to help you locate the exact phrase you need, when you need it. You'll also gain the confidence to go beyond what is in the book, as you can adapt the phrases by using the dictionary section to substitute your own words.

The **Gem Phrasebook and Dictionary** includes:
• Over 60 topics arranged thematically, so that you can easily find an expression to suit the situation

• Simple pronunciation which accompanies each word and phrase, to make sure you are understood when speaking aloud

• Tips to safeguard against any cultural faux pas, providing the essential dos and don'ts of local customs or etiquette

• A basic grammar section which will help you to build on your phrases

• **FACE TO FACE** dialogue sections to give you a flavour of what to expect from a real conversation

• A handy map of the country which shows the major cities and how to pronounce them

• **YOU MAY HEAR** sections for common announcements and messages, so that you don't miss important information when out and about

- A user-friendly 3000 word dictionary to ensure you'll never be stuck for something to say

- **LIFELINE** phrases are listed on the inside covers for quick reference. These basic words and phrases will be essential to your time abroad

Before you jet off, it's worth spending time looking through the topics to see what is covered and becoming familiar with pronunciation.

The colour key below shows you how to search the phrasebook by theme, so you'll be able to find relevant phrases very quickly.

Talking to people

Getting around

Staying somewhere

Shopping

Leisure

Communications

Practicalities

Health

Eating out

Menu reader

Reference

Grammar

Dictionary

Contents

Pronouncing Greek

Greek alphabet

Greek is spelt exactly as it sounds. The only difficulty may occur with letters which have the same sound, e.g. **υ**, **η**, **ι** or **ει**, **οι** and with double consonants. The names of the 24 letters of the Greek alphabet are given below:

			sound
α, Α	άλφα	alfa	ah
β, Β	βήτα	veeta	v
γ, Γ	γάμα	ghama	gh
δ, Δ	δέλτα	dhelta	dh
ε, Ε	έψιλον	epseelon	eh
ζ, Ζ	ζήτα	zeeta	z
η, Η	ήτα	eeta	ee
θ, Θ	θήτα	theeta	th
ι, Ι	γιώτα	yota	ee
κ, Κ	κάπα	kapa	k
λ, Λ	λάμδα	lamdha	l
μ, Μ	μι	mee	m
ν, Ν	νι	nee	n

			sound
ξ, Ξ	ξι	ksee	ks
o, O	όμικρον	omeekron	oh
π, Π	πι	pee	p
ρ, P	ρο	ro	r
σ, ς, Σ	σίγμα	seeghma	s
τ, T	ταυ	taf	t
υ, Y	ύψιλον	eepseelon	ee
φ, Φ	φι	fee	f
χ, X	χι	khee	kh
ψ, Ψ	ψι	psee	ps
ω, Ω	ωμέγα	omegha	oh

In the pronunciation system used here, Greek sounds are represented by spellings of the nearest possible sounds in English. When you read the pronunciation guide, pronounce the letters as if reading English. The **bold** shows where the stress falls in the word (in the Greek script it is marked with an accent).

	remarks	example	pronunciation
gh	like **r** at back of throat	**γάλα**	**gh**ala
	where **γ** is followed by **ι** or **ε**, it's	**για**	(ya)
dh	like **th** in this	**δάχτυλο**	**dh**akhteelo
th	like **th** in thin	**θέατρο**	**th**eatro
ks	like **x** in fox	**ξένος**	**ks**enos
r	slightly trilled **r**	**ρόδα**	**r**odha
kh	like **ch** in loch	**χάνω**	**kh**ano
	or like a rough **h**	**χέρι**	**kh**eree

Here are a few tricky letter combinations:

αι	e	met	**γυναίκα**	yeen**e**ka
αυ	af	caf**é**	**αυτό**	af**to**
	av	h**av**e	**αύριο**	**a**vreeo
ει	ee	m**ee**t	**είκοσι**	**ee**kosee
ευ	ef	**ef**fect	**Δευτέρα**	dhef**te**ra
	ev	**ev**ery	**Ευρώπη**	**ev**ropee
γγ	ng	ha**ng**	**Αγγλία**	angl**ee**a
γκ	g	**g**et	**γκάζι**	**g**azee
	ng	ha**ng**	**άγκυρα**	**a**ngeera

9

ντ	nd	ha**nd**	**αντίο**	a**nd**eeo
	d	**d**og	**ντομάτα**	**d**omata
μπ	b	**b**ag	**μπλούζα**	**b**looza
οι	ee	m**ee**t	**πλοίο**	pl**ee**o
ου	oo	m**oo**n	**ούζο**	**oo**zo

The letters **η**, **ι**, **υ**, **οι**, and **ει** have the same sound **ee** and **αι** and **ε** have the same sound **e** (as in m<u>e</u>t). You should also note that the Greek question mark is a semi-colon, i.e. ;.

Top ten tips

....

1   Don't wear beachwear anywhere but at the beach.

2   'Yes' is signified by a slight downward nod of the head; 'no' is a slight upward nod of the head.

3   Nodding your head to indicate 'yes' is not polite; say 'yes' instead.

4   One of the rudest gestures is to thrust the palm of your hand in front of someone's face.

5   Online gambling is illegal in internet cafés and in public.

6   Be prepared to be asked about your age, your marital status, etc. Personal questions are commonplace and are not considered rude.

7   Easter is celebrated more than Christmas.

8   Codeine is available on prescription only, so medicines containing codeine should not be brought into Greece.

9   If your passport is stolen, call the tourist police first and they can often act as translators.

10 Names are attached to particular days of the year. For example, if you are called Elena you will celebrate your name day on May 21st. Name day celebrations are as important as birthdays!

Talking to people

Hello/goodbye, yes/no

There are two forms of address in Greek, formal and informal. Greek people use the formal until they are on a first name basis.

Yes	**Ναι**	ne
No	**Όχι**	okhee
OK	**Εντάξει**	endaksee
Please	**Παρακαλώ**	parakalo
Don't mention it	**Παρακαλώ**	parakalo
Excuse me!/ Sorry!	**Συγνώμη!**	seeghnomee!
Thank you	**Ευχαριστώ**	efkhareesto
Thanks very much	**Ευχαριστώ πολύ**	efkhareesto polee

13

Sir/Mr	**Κύριε**
	keeree-e
Madam/Mrs/Ms	**Κυρία**
	keereea
Miss	**Δεσποινίς**
	dhespeenees

Hello/	**Γεια σας** (formal)
Goodbye	ya sas
	Γεια σου (informal)
	ya soo
Hello	**Χαίρετε**
	kherete
Goodbye	**Αντίο**
	andeeo
Good morning	**Καλημέρα**
	kaleemera
Good evening	**Καλησπέρα**
	kaleespera
Good night	**Καληνύχτα**
	kaleeneekhta
How are you?	**Τι κάνετε;** (formal)
	tee kanete?
	Τι κάνεις; (informal)
	tee kanees?
Very well	**Πολύ καλά**
	polee kala
And you?	**Εσείς;**
	esees?

I don't understand	**Δεν καταλαβαίνω** dhen katalaveno
Do you understand?	**Καταλαβαίνετε;** katalavenete?
Do you speak English?	**Μιλάτε αγγλικά;** meelate angleeka?
I speak very little Greek	**Μιλάω πολύ λίγα ελληνικά** meelao polee leegha eleeneeka

Key phrases

. . . .

The easiest way to ask for something is by naming what you want and adding the word for please, **parakalo**.

the (masculine)	**o** o
(feminine)	**η** ee
(neuter)	**το** to
the coffee	**ο καφές** o kafes
the beer	**η μπύρα** ee beera
the glass	**το ποτήρι** to poteeree

a/one coffee	**ένας καφές** **e**nas kaf**e**s
a/one beer	**μία μπύρα** m**ee**a b**ee**ra
a/one glass	**ένα ποτήρι** **e**na pot**ee**ree
a coffee, please	**έναν καφέ, παρακαλώ** **e**nan kaf**e** parakal**o**
a beer, please	**μία μπύρα, παρακαλώ** m**ee**a b**ee**ra parakal**o**
a glass of wine, please	**ένα ποτήρι κρασί,** **παρακαλώ** **e**na pot**ee**ree kras**ee** parakal**o**
my passport	**το διαβατήριό μου** to dheeavat**ee**ree**o** moo
my room	**το δωμάτιό μου** to dhom**a**tee**o** moo
I'd like...	**Θα ήθελα...** tha **ee**thela...
I'd like an ice cream	**Θα ήθελα ένα παγωτό** tha **ee**thela **e**na paghot**o**
We'd like...	**Θα θέλαμε...** tha th**e**lame...
We'd like two rooms	**Θα θέλαμε δύο δωμάτια** tha th**e**lame dh**ee**o dhom**a**teea

We'd like to go to Athens	**Θα θέλαμε να πάμε στην Αθήνα**	
	tha th**e**lame na p**a**me steen ath**ee**na	
Do you have...?	**Έχετε...;**	
	ekhete...?	
Do you have bread?	**Έχετε ψωμί;**	
	ekhete psom**ee**?	
Do you have milk?	**Έχετε γάλα;**	
	ekhete gh**a**la?	
How much is it?	**Πόσο κάνει;**	
	p**o**so k**a**nee?	
How much does ... cost?	**Πόσο κοστίζει ο/η/το...;**	
	p**o**so kost**ee**zee o/ee/to...?	
How much is the wine?	**Πόσο κάνει το κρασί;**	
	p**o**so k**a**nee to kras**ee**?	
How much does the ticket cost?	**Πόσο κοστίζει το εισιτήριο;**	
	p**o**so kost**ee**zee to eeseet**ee**reeo?	
large	**μεγάλο**	
	megh**a**lo	
small	**μικρό**	
	meekr**o**	
with	**με**	
	me	
without	**χωρίς**	
	khor**ee**s	
Where is...?	**Πού είναι...;**	
	poo **ee**ne...?	

Where is the toilet?	**Πού είναι η τουαλέτα;** poo **ee**ne ee tooal**e**ta?
Where is the nearest bank?	**Πού είναι η κοντινότερη τράπεζα;** poo **ee**ne ee kondeen**o**teree tr**a**peza?
When does it open?	**Πότε ανοίγει;** p**o**te an**ee**yee?
When does it close?	**Πότε κλείνει;** p**o**te kl**ee**nee?
today	**σήμερα** s**ee**mera
tonight	**απόψε** ap**o**pse
tomorrow	**αύριο** **a**vreeo
yesterday	**χθες** khthes
Can I...?	**Μπορώ να...;** bor**o** na...?
Can I pay?	**Μπορώ να πληρώσω;** bor**o** na pleer**o**so?

Signs and notices

ανοικτό	open
κλειστό	closed
σελφ σερβις	self-service
είσοδος	entrance
έξοδος	exit
ταμείο	cash desk
ωθήσατε	push
σύρατε	pull
τουαλέτες	toilets
κέντρο	centre
ανδρών	gents
γυναικών	ladies
δεν λειτουργεί	out of order
κατειλημμένο	engaged
πληροφορίες	information
ενοικιάζεται	for hire/to rent
πωλείται	for sale
εκπτώσεις	sales
δωμάτια	rooms

μουσείο	museum
ιδιωτικός χώρος	private
ημερομηνία	date
μην αγγίζετε	do not touch
απαγορεύεται το μπάνιο	no bathing
απαγορεύεται η είσοδος	no entry
καπνίζοντες	smoking
απαγορεύεται το κάπνισμα	no smoking
απαγορεύεται η στάθμευση	no parking
απαγορεύεται η κατασκήνωση	no camping
απαγορεύεται η είσοδος	no entry
ισόγειο	ground floor
εισιτήρια	tickets
ΕΟΤ	Greek Tourist Office
φύλαξη αποσκευών	left luggage

Polite expressions

• •

Don't worry about making mistakes. Greek people appreciate any attempt at speaking their language. You will often be greeted with **kalos eerthate**, meaning welcome.

The meal was delicious	**Το φαγητό ήταν νοστιμότατο** to fa-yeet**o ee**tan nosteem**o**tato
Thank you very much	**Σας ευχαριστώ πολύ** sas efkhareest**o** pol**ee**
This is a gift for you	**Είναι ένα δώρο για σας** **ee**ne **e**na dh**o**ro ya sas
Pleased to meet you	**Χάρηκα για τη γνωριμία** kh**a**reeka ya tee ghnoreem**ee**a
This is my husband	**Από 'δω ο σύζυγός μου** ap**o** dho o s**ee**zeegh**o**s moo
This is my wife	**Από 'δω η σύζυγός μου** ap**o** dho ee s**ee**zeegh**o**s moo

Celebrations

- -

I wish you a...	**Σας εύχομαι...** sas **e**fkhome...
I wish you a... (informal)	**Σου εύχομαι...** soo **e**fkhome...
Merry Christmas!	**Καλά Χριστούγεννα** kal**a** khreest**oo**yena
Happy New Year!	**Καλή χρονιά** kal**ee** khrony**a**
Happy birthday!	**Χρόνια πολλά** khr**o**nya pol**a**
Cheers!	**γεια μας!** ya mas!

Making friends

- -

In this section we have used the informal form for the questions.

FACE TO FACE

Πώς σε λένε;
p**o**s se l**e**ne?
What's your name?

Με λένε...
me lene...
My name is...

Από πού είσαι;
apo poo eese?
Where are you from?

Είμαι Άγγλος από το Λονδίνο
eeme anglos apo to londheeno
I am English, from London

Χάρηκα!
khareeka!
Pleased to meet you!

How old are you?	**Πόσων χρονών είσαι;** poson khronon eese?	
I'm ... years old	**Είμαι ... χρονών** eeme ... khronon	
Are you from Greece?	**Είσαι από την Ελλάδα;** eese apo teen eladha?	
I'm from...	**Είμαι από την...** eeme apo teen...	
England/English	**Αγγλία/Αγγλικά** angleea/angleeka	
Scotland/ Scottish	**Σκοτία/Σκοτσέζικα** skoteea/skotsezeeka	
Wales/Welsh	**Ουαλία/Ουαλικά** ooaleea/ooaleeka	

23

Ireland/Irish	**Ιρλανδία/Ιρλανδικά** eerlandh**ee**a/eerlandh**e**zeeka
USA/American	**Ηνωμένες Πολιτείες** **Αμερικής/Αμερικάνικα** eenom**e**nes poleet**ee**yes amereek**ee**s/amereek**a**neeka
Australia/ Australian	**Αυστραλία/Αυστραλέζικα** afstral**ee**a/afstral**e**zeeka
Where do you live?	**Πού μένεις;** poo m**e**nees?
Where do you live? (plural)	**Πού μένετε;** poo m**e**nete
I live in London	**Ζω στο Λονδίνο** zo sto londh**ee**no
We live in Glasgow	**Ζούμε στη Γλασκώβη** z**oo**me stee ghlask**o**vee
I work	**Εργάζομαι** ergh**a**zome
I'm retired	**Είμαι συνταξιούχος** **ee**me seendaksee**oo**khos
I'm...	**Είμαι...** **ee**me...
single	**ελεύθερος(-η)** el**e**fther-os(-ee)
married	**παντρεμένος(-η)** pandrem**e**n-os(-ee)
I have...	**Έχω...** ekho...

a boyfriend	**ένα φίλο** **e**na f**ee**lo
a girlfriend	**μία φίλη** m**ee**a f**ee**lee
I have ... children	**Έχω ... παιδιά** **e**kho ... pedhy**a**
I have no children	**Δεν έχω παιδιά** dhen **e**kho pedhy**a**
I'm here...	**Βρίσκομαι εδώ...** vr**ee**skome edh**o**...
on holiday	**για διακοπές** ya dheeakop**es**
for work	**για δουλειά** ya dhoolya

Work

. . . .

What work do you do?	**Τι δουλειά κάνετε;** tee dhooly**a** k**a**nete?
Do you enjoy it?	**Σας αρέσει;** sas ar**e**see?
I'm...	**Είμαι...** **ee**me...
a doctor	**γιατρός** yatr**os**
a teacher (male/female)	**δάσκαλος/δασκάλα** dh**a**skalos/dhask**a**la

25

Weather

Talking to people

It's sunny	**Έχει ήλιο** **e**khee **ee**lyo
It's very hot	**Κάνει πολύ ζέστη** ka nee pol**ee** z**e**stee
It's windy	**Έχει αέρα** **e**khee a**e**ra
What awful weather!	**Τι απαίσιος καιρός!** tee ap**e**seeos ker**o**s!
What will the weather be like tomorrow?	**Τι καιρό θα κάνει αύριο;** tee ker**o** tha k**a**nee **a**vreeo?
What is the temperature?	**Τι θερμοκρασία έχει;** tee thermokras**ee**a **e**khee?

Getting around

Asking the way

απέναντι ap**e**nantee	opposite
δίπλα στο/στην dh**ee**pla sto/steen	next to
κοντά στο/στην kond**a** sto/steen	near to
φανάρια fan**a**rya	traffic lights
στη γωνία stee ghon**ee**a	at the corner
στην πλατεία steen plat**ee**a	in the square

FACE TO FACE

Με συγχωρείτε! Πώς θα πάω στο σταθμό;
me seenkhor**ee**te! p**o**s tha p**a**o sto stathm**o**?
Excuse me, how do I get to the station?

Όλο ευθεία και μετά την εκκλησία στρίψτε αριστερά/δεξιά.
olo efth**ee**a ke met**a** teen eklees**ee**a str**i**pste areester**a**/dhekseе**a**.
Keep straight on, after the church turn left/right.

27

Είναι μακριά;
eene makree**a**?
Is it far?

Όχι, περίπου 400 μ/πέντε λεπτά
okhi, per**ee**pou 400 m./p**e**nte lept**a**
No, 400 metres/five minutes

Ευχαριστώ!
efkharist**o**!
Thank you!

Παρακαλώ
parakal**o**
You're welcome

I'm looking for...	**ψάχνω για…** ps**a**khno ya...
Can I walk there?	**Μπορώ να πάω με τα πόδια;** bor**o** na p**a**o me ta p**o**dhya?
We're lost	**Έχουμε χαθεί** **e**khoome khath**ee**
Is this the way to...?	**Πάω καλά για…;** p**a**o kal**a** ya...?
Is it far?	**Είναι μακριά;** **ee**ne makree**a**?
How do I get onto the motorway?	**Πώς θα βγω στην εθνική οδό;** p**o**s tha vgho steen ethneek**ee** odh**o**?
Can you show me where it is on the map?	**Μπορείτε να μου το δείξετε στον χάρτη;** bor**ee**te na moo to dh**ee**ksete p**a**no ston kh**a**rtee?

Στρίψτε δεξιά/αριστερά streepste dhekseea/ areestera	Turn right/left
Προχωρήστε ευθεία μέχρι να φτάσετε... prokhoreeste eftheea mekhree na ftasete...	Keep straight on until you get...
στη διασταύρωση stee dheeastavrosee	to the junction

Getting around

Bus and coach

Bus is the major form of overland transport in Greece and Cyprus. There is a good network of local and long-distance routes. On some routes you must buy a ticket before you depart.

FACE TO FACE

Συγνώμη, ποιο λεωφορείο πάει στο κέντρο;
seeghnomee, pyo leoforeeo paee sto kentro?
Excuse me, which bus goes to the centre?

Το νούμερο 15
to noomero 15
Number 15

Πού είναι η στάση;
poo **ee**ne ee st**a**see?
Where is the bus stop?

Εκεί δεξιά
ek**ee** dheks**ee**a
There, on the right

Πού μπορώ να αγοράσω εισιτήρια;
poo bor**o** na aghor**a**so eeseet**ee**reea?
Where can I buy tickets?

Στο περίπτερο
sto per**ee**ptero
At the kiosk

Is there a bus to...?	**Υπάρχει λεωφορείο για...;** eep**a**rkhee leofor**ee**o ya...?
Where do I catch the bus to...?	**Από πού θα πάρω το λεωφορείο για...;** ap**o** poo tha p**a**ro to leofor**ee**o ya...?
A child's ticket	**Ένα παιδικό εισιτήριο** **e**na pedheek**o** eeseet**ee**reeo
How much is it...?	**Πόσο κάνει...;** p**o**so k**a**nee...?
to the beach	**για τη θάλασσα** ya tee th**a**lasa
to the airport	**για το αεροδρόμιο** ya to aerodhr**o**meeo
How often are the buses to...?	**Κάθε πότε έχει λεωφορείο για...;** k**a**the p**o**te **e**khee leofor**ee**o ya...?

30

When is	**Πότε είναι**	
	pote **ee**ne	
the first	**το πρώτο**	
	to pr**o**to	
the last	**το τελευταίο**	
	to telef**te**o	
bus	**λεωφορείο**	
	leofor**ee**o	
coach	**το τουριστικό λεωφορείο**	
	to tooreesteek**o** leofor**ee**o	
shuttle bus	**το λεωφορείο κλειστής**	
	διαδρομής	
	to leofor**ee**o kleest**ee**s	
	dheeadrom**ee**s	
to...?	**για...;**	
	ya...?	
Please can you tell me when to get off?	**Παρακαλώ, μπορείτε να μου πείτε πότε να κατέβω;**	
	parakal**o** bor**ee**te na moo p**ee**te p**o**te na kat**e**vo?	

YOU MAY HEAR...

Το λεωφορείο αυτό δε σταματά στο... to leofor**ee**o aft**o** dhe stamat**a** sto...	This bus doesn't stop in...
Πρέπει να πάρετε το... pr**e**pee na p**a**rete to...	You have to catch the...

Metro

• •

There is a metro network under construction in Thessaloniki, scheduled to be finished in 2018. The metro system in Athens opens at 5.30 a.m. and closes at midnight. There is a 3-day tourist ticket for all modes of transport which includes a return to/from the airport. You can also get a 24-hour ticket. There are armed police on patrol at stations. It is forbidden to eat or drink in the stations and on the metro.

Where is the metro station?	**Πού είναι ο σταθμός του μετρό;** poo **ee**ne o stathm**o**s too metr**o**?
(for old electric line)	**του ηλεκτρικού;** too eelektreek**oo**?
A ticket	**Ένα εισιτήριο** **e**na eeseet**ee**reeo
A 24-hour ticket	**Ένα ημερήσιο εισιτήριο** **e**na eemer**ee**seeo eeseet**ee**reeo
4 tickets, please	**Τέσσερα εισιτήρια παρακαλώ** t**e**sera eeseet**ee**reea parakal**o**
Do you have an underground map?	**Έχετε έναν χάρτη με τις γραμμές του μετρό;** **e**khete **e**nan kh**a**rtee me tees ghramm**e**s too metr**o**?
I want to go to...	**Θέλω να πάω στο/στη...** th**e**lo na p**a**o sto/stee...

Do I have to change?	**Πρέπει να αλλάξω τρένο;**
	prepee na al**a**kso tr**e**no?
Where?	**Πού;**
	poo?
Which line do I take?	**Ποια γραμμή πρέπει να πάρω;**
	pya ghramm**ee** pr**e**pee na p**a**ro?

Train

Train services in Greece are limited and slow in comparison with other western European railways. There is only one main line, operated by Greek Railways **ΟΣΕ**, running from Athens north to Thessaloniki and onwards to Bulgaria (Sofia), Macedonia (Skopje) and Serbia (Belgrade). The Peloponnese is served by a narrow-gauge line from Athens. There are also 3 suburban lines operated by **TRAINOSE**, which link the three major cities, Athens, Thessaloniki and Patras with their suburbs. There are no trains in Cyprus.

FACE TO FACE

Πότε έχει τρένο για...;
pote **e**khei tr**e**no ya...?
When is the train to...?

Στις πέντε και δέκα
stees p**e**nte ke dh**e**ka
At ten past five

Θα ήθελα δύο εισιτήρια παρακαλώ
tha **ee**thela dh**ee**o eeseet**ee**reea parakal**o**
I'd like two tickets, please

Απλό εισιτήριο ή με επιστροφή;
apl**o** eeseet**ee**reeo **ee** me epeestrof**ee**?
Single or return?

Where is the train station?	**Πού είναι ο σταθμός τρένου;** poo **ee**ne o stathm**o**s tr**e**noo?
To the station, please	**Στο σταθμό παρακαλώ** sto stathm**o** parakal**o**
A single to...	**Ένα απλό εισιτήριο για...** **e**na apl**o** eeseet**ee**reeo ya...
Two singles to...	**Δύο απλά εισιτήρια για...** dh**ee**o apl**a** eeseet**ee**reea ya...
A return to...	**Ένα εισιτήριο με επιστροφή για...** **e**na eeseet**ee**reeo me epeestrof**ee** ya...
Two return tickets to...	**Δύο εισιτήρια με επιστροφή για...** dh**ee**o eeseet**ee**reea me epeestrof**ee** ya...
economy class	**Τουριστική θέση** tooreesteek**ee** th**e**see
e-ticket	**το ηλεκτρονικό εισιτήριο** t**o** eelektroneek**o** eeseet**ee**reeo
e-booking	**η ηλεκτονική κράτηση** ee eelektroneek**ee** kr**a**teesee

I want to book a seat to Thessaloniki	**Θέλω να κλείσω ένα εισιτήριο για τη Θεσσαλονίκη** thelo na kleeso ena eeseeteereeo ya tee thesaloneekee
When does it arrive in...?	**Πότε φτάνει στο...;** pote ftanee sto...?
Do I have to change?	**Πρέπει να αλλάξω;** prepee na alakso?
Where?	**Πού;** poo?
Which platform does it leave from?	**Από ποια πλατφόρμα φεύγει;** apo pya platforma fevyee?
Is this the train for...?	**Αυτό είναι το τρένο για...;** afto eene to treno ya...?
When will it leave?	**Πότε θα φύγει;** pote tha feeyee?
I booked online	**Έκανα κράτηση μέσω διαδικτύου** ekana krateesee meso dheeadheekteeoo
Does the train stop at...?	**Σταματάει το τρένο στο...;** stamataee to treno sto...?
Please let me know when we get to...	**Μου λέτε, σας παρακαλώ, πότε φτάνουμε στο...** moo lete, sas parakalo, pote ftanoome sto...

Is this free? (seat)	**Είναι ελεύθερη;**
	eene el**e**ftheree?
Excuse me	**Με συγχωρείτε**
	me seenkhor**ee**te

Taxi

• •

Taxis in Greece are a relatively cheap form of transport in big cities. Yellow city cabs are metered, with rates doubling between midnight and 5 a.m. If you get a taxi from an airport, bus/train station or a port, there is an additional fee. You will also be charged for each piece of luggage over 10kg. In smaller towns, taxis are grey or blue and do not have meters. Check the fare with the driver in advance. Taxi drivers are obliged to provide the client with a receipt. If you have a complaint, you can report it to the tourist police.

I need a taxi	**Χρειάζομαι ταξί**
	khree**a**zome taks**ee**
Where can I get a taxi?	**Πού μπορώ να πάρω ένα ταξί;**
	poo bor**o** na p**a**ro **e**na taks**ee**?
How much is a taxi...?	**Πόσο κάνει το ταξί...;**
	p**o**so k**a**nee to taks**ee**...?
to the station	**για το σταθμό**
	ya to stathm**o**

to the airport	**για το αεροδρόμιο**
	ya to aerodhr**o**meeo
to the centre	**για το κέντρο**
	ya to k**e**ntro
Please take me (us) to...	**Παρακαλώ πηγαίνετέ με (μας) στο...**
	parakal**o** peey**e**net**e** me (mas) sto...
Keep the change	**Κρατήστε τα ρέστα**
	krat**ee**ste ta r**e**sta
Sorry, I don't have change	**Συγνώμη, δεν έχω ψιλά**
	seeghn**o**mee, dhen **e**kho pseel**a**

Boat and ferry

In Greece, with its many islands, ferries are an important means of transport. There are several local ferries and speed boats operating to and from most islands. They are well-connected to large cities, such as Athens and Thessaloniki, as well as remote beaches. Island hopping is essential if you want to experience an authentic Greek summer! The centre of the ferry network is the port of Piraeus. Hydrofoils – **ιπτάμενο δελφίνι** (eept**a**meno dhelf**ee**nee) 'flying dolphins' – operate between Piraeus and the nearer islands.

When is the next boat to...?	**Πότε φεύγει το επόμενο πλοίο για...;** pote fevyee to epomeno pleeo ya...?
Have you a timetable?	**Έχετε πρόγραμμα με τα δρομολόγια;** ekhete proghrama me ta dhromoloya?
Is there a boat to...?	**Υπάρχει πλοίο για...;** eeparkhee pleeo ya...?
How much is a ticket?	**Πόσο κάνει ένα εισιτήριο;** poso kanee ena eeseeteereeo?
single	**απλό** aplo
return	**με επιστροφή** me epeestrofee
How long is the journey?	**Πόσο διαρκεί το ταξίδι;** poso dheearkee to takseedhee?
What time do we get to...?	**Τι ώρα φτάνουμε στο...;** tee ora ftanoome sto...?
Where does the boat leave from?	**Από πού φεύγει το πλοίο;** apo poo fevyee to pleeo?
When is...?	**Πότε είναι...;** pote eene...?
the first...	**το πρώτο...** to proto...

the last...	**το τελευταίο...**
	to teleft**eo**...
hydrofoil	**ιπτάμενο δελφίνι**
	eept**a**meno dhelf**ee**nee
boat	**πλοίο**
	pl**ee**o
ferry	**φεριμπότ**
	fereeb**o**t

Air travel

· ·

The major airports in Greece are **Eleftherios Venizelos** (Athens), **Nikos Kazantzakis** (Iraklio, Crete) and **Macedonia International Airport** in Thessaloniki. If you are arriving in Athens on a non-Greek carrier and have a domestic flight to catch, allow plenty of time to get across the airport. Greece is highly security-conscious and it is against the law to take photographs of airports.

αφίξεις af**ee**ksees	arrivals
είσοδος eesodhos	entrance
έξοδος eksodhos	exit
αναχωρήσεις anakhor**ee**sees	departures

πτήση pt**ee**see	flight
η παραδιδόμενη αποσκευή ee paradheedh**o**menee aposkev**ee**	checked luggage
η χειραποσκευή ee kheeraposkev**ee**	hand luggage
απαγορεύονται τα υγρά apaghor**e**vonte ta eeghr**a**	no liquids

Your luggage exceeds the maximum weight	**Οι αποσκευές σας ξεπερνούν το επιτρεπόμενο βάρος** ee aposkev**e**s sas ksepern**oo**n to epeetrep**o**meno v**a**ros
To the airport, please	**Στο αεροδρόμιο, παρακαλώ** sto aerodhr**o**meeo, parakal**o**
How do I get to the airport?	**Πώς μπορώ να πάω στο αεροδρόμιο;** pos bor**o** na p**a**o sto aerodhr**o**meeo?
Is there a bus to the city centre?	**Υπάρχει λεωφορείο για το κέντρο της πόλης;** eep**a**rkhee leofor**ee**o ya to k**e**ndro tees p**o**lees?
Where do I check in for... (airline)?	**Πού γίνεται ο έλεγχος αποσκευών για…;** poo y**ee**nete o **e**lengkhos aposkev**o**n ya…?

Which gate is it for the flight to…?	**Ποια είναι η έξοδος της πτήσης για…;**
	pya **ee**ne ee **e**ksodhos tees pt**ee**sees ya…?
Where can I print my ticket?	**Πού μπορώ να εκτυπώσω το εισητήριό μου;**
	poo bor**o** na ekteep**o**so to eeseet**ee**reeo moo?
I have my boarding pass on my smartphone	**Έχω την κάρτα επιβίβασης στο έξυπνο τηλέφωνό μου**
	ekho teen k**a**rta epeev**ee**vasees sto **e**kseepno teel**e**fono moo

Customs control

• •

You will not be allowed to enter Greece or Cyprus if your passport has a stamp from the Turkish Republic of Northern Cyprus. You will need an export permit if you plan to take home any antiquities, including old icons, regardless of their value. Illegal export of antiquities is considered a very serious crime. With the single European market, passengers arriving from an EU member state are subject only to occasional checks and can go through the blue customs channel.

| Do I have to pay duty on this? | **Πρέπει να πληρώσω φόρο γι' αυτό;** |
| | pr**e**pee na pleer**o**so f**o**ro yaft**o**? |

| It is for my own personal use | **Είναι για προσωπική μου χρήση**
eene ya prosopeek**ee** moo khr**ee**see |
| We are on our way to... | **Πηγαίνουμε για...**
peeg**e**noome ya... |

Car hire

· ·

Hiring a car is easy as international companies have branches in Athens and other major cities. Local companies in smaller towns and on the islands also offer good deals. The minimum driving age in Greece is 18 but most rental agencies require you to be 21 or 23 to hire larger vehicles.

| **το δίπλωμα οδήγησης**
to dh**ee**ploma odh**ee**yeesees | driving licence |
| **η όπισθεν** ee **o**peesthen | reverse gear |

| I want to hire a car | **Θέλω να νοικιάσω ένα αυτοκίνητο**
th**e**lo na neeky**a**so **e**na aftok**ee**neeto |
| for ... days | **για ... μέρες**
ya ... m**e**res |

42

How much is it...?	**Πόσο κάνει...;** poso kanee...?
per day	**τη μέρα** tee mera
per week	**τη βδομάδα** tee vdhomadha
How much is the deposit?	**Πόση είναι η προκαταβολή;** posee eene ee prokatavolee?
Is there a charge per kilometre?	**Γίνεται χρέωση ανά χιλιόμετρο;** yeenete khreosee ana kheelyometro?
What is included in the insurance?	**Τι περιλαμβάνεται στην ασφάλεια;** tee pereelamvanete steen asfaleea?
Do I have to return the car here?	**Πρέπει να γυρίσω το αυτοκίνητο εδώ;** prepee na yeereeso to aftokeeneeto edho?
What time?	**Τι ώρα;** tee ora?
I'd like to leave it in...	**Θα ήθελα να το αφήσω στο...** tha eethela na to afeeso sto...
What do I do if I break down?	**Τι θα κάνω αν μείνω από βλάβη;** tee tha kano an meeno apo vlavee?

Μπορείτε να γυρίσετε το αυτοκίνητο με άδειο ρεζερβουάρ bor**ee**te na yeer**ee**sete to aftok**ee**neeto me **a**dheeo rezervoo**ar**	You can return the car with an empty tank

Motorbike hire

Hiring a motorbike is a popular and economical form of transport in both Greece and Cyprus. A licence is required to ride motorcycles from 50cc and above. Regulations requiring the wearing of crash helmets are widely flouted. When hiring, check that the machine is mechanically sound and that insurance is provided.

I want to hire...	**Θέλω να νοικιάσω...** th**e**lo na neeky**a**so...
a motorcycle	**μοτοσυκλέτα** motoseekl**e**ta
a moped	**μοτοποδήλατο** motopodh**ee**lato
for a day	**για μία μέρα** ya m**ee**a m**e**ra
for the morning	**για το πρωί** ya to pro**ee**

Getting around

for the afternoon	**για το απόγευμα** ya to ap**o**yevma
Is a crash helmet included in the price?	**Το κράνος περιλαμβάνεται στην τιμή;** to kr**a**nos pereelamv**a**nete steen teem**ee**?
Is insurance included in the price?	**Η ασφάλιση περιλαμβάνεται στην τιμή;** ee asf**a**leesee pereelamv**a**nete steen teem**ee**?

Driving

• •

Try to avoid driving in the major cities, particularly Athens. Traffic congestion can be appalling and parking in city centres almost impossible. Drive on the right in Greece but on the left in Cyprus.

Can I park here?	**Μπορώ να παρκάρω εδώ;** bor**o** na park**a**ro edh**o**?
Where can I park?	**Πού μπορώ να παρκάρω;** poo bor**o** na park**a**ro?
Do I need a parking ticket?	**Χρειάζομαι κάρτα στάθμευσης;** khree**a**zome k**a**rta st**a**thmefsees?
We're going to...	**Πηγαίνουμε στο...** peey**e**noome sto...

| Which junction is it for...? | Σε ποια διασταύρωση είναι...; |
| | se pya dheeast**a**vrosee **ee**ne...? |

Petrol

αμόλυβδη amoleevdhee	unleaded
πετρέλαιο petreleo	diesel
βενζίνη venzeenee	petrol

Is there a petrol station near here?	Υπάρχει βενζινάδικο εδώ κοντά;
	eep**a**rkhee venzeen**a**dheeko edh**o** kond**a**?
Fill it up, please	Γεμίστε το, παρακαλώ
	yem**ee**ste to parakal**o**
Please check the oil/the water	Παρακαλώ ελέγξτε τα λάδια/το νερό
	parakal**o** el**e**nkste ta l**a**dhya/ to ner**o**
20 euros worth of unleaded petrol	Είκοσι ευρώ αμόλυβδη βενζίνη
	eekosee evr**o** am**o**leevdhee venz**ee**nee
Where is...?	Πού είναι...;
	poo **ee**ne...?
the air line	η παροχή του αέρα
	ee parokh**ee** too a**e**ra

the water	**το νερό**
	to ner**o**
Please check the tyres	**Παρακαλώ ελέγξτε τα λάστιχα**
	parakal**o** el**e**nkste ta l**a**steekha

Breakdown

. . . .

Can you help me?	**Μπορείτε να με βοηθήσετε;**
	bor**ee**te na me voeeth**ee**sete?
My car has broken down	**Το αυτοκίνητό μου χάλασε**
	to aftok**ee**neet**o** moo kh**a**lase
Is there a garage near here?	**Υπάρχει συνεργείο εδώ κοντά;**
	eep**a**rkhee seenery**ee**o edh**o** kond**a**?
The car won't start	**Το αυτοκίνητο δεν ξεκινά**
	to aftok**ee**neeto dhen ksekeen**a**
Can you give me a push?	**Μπορείτε να σπρώξετε;**
	bor**ee**te na spr**o**ksete?
I've run out of petrol	**Έμεινα από βενζίνη**
	emeena ap**o** venz**ee**nee
Can you tow me to the nearest garage?	**Μπορείτε να με τραβήξετε μέχρι το κοντινότερο συνεργείο;**
	bor**ee**te na me trav**ee**ksete m**e**khree to kondeen**o**tero seenery**ee**o?

47

Car parts

The ... doesn't work	ο/η/το ... δε λειτουργεί o/ee/to ... dhe leetooryee	
The ... don't work	οι/τα ... δε λειτουργούν ee/ta ... dhe leetoorghoon	
accelerator	το γκάζι	gazee
battery	η μπαταρία	batareea
brakes	τα φρένα	frena
choke	το τσοκ	tsok
clutch	ο συμπλέκτης	seemblektees
engine	η μηχανή	meekhanee
exhaust pipe	η εξάτμιση	eksatmeesee
fuse	η ασφάλεια	asfaleea
gears	οι ταχύτητες	takheeteetes
handbrake	το χειρόφρενο	kheerofreno
headlights	τα φώτα	ta fota
ignition	η ανάφλεξη	anafleksee
indicator	το φλας	flas
radiator	το ψυγείο	pseeyeeo
rear lights	τα πίσω φώτα	peeso fota
seat belt	η ζώνη ασφαλείας	zonee asfaleeas

spare wheel	η ρεζέρβα	rez**e**rva
spark plug	το μπουζί	booz**ee**
steering wheel	το τιμόνι	teem**o**nee
tyre	το λάστιχο	l**a**steekho
wheel	η ρόδα	r**o**dha
windscreen	το παρμπρίζ	parbr**ee**z
windscreen wiper	ο υαλοκα-θαριστήρας	eealokatharee-st**ee**ras

Road signs

camping

customs control

restricted parking
zone

end to restricted
parking zone

directional sign

north

W e s t

e a s t

south

no parking in
odd-numbered
months

no parking in
even-numbered
months

motorway toll

parking for
card holders

Speed limits in Greece
are in kilometres

parking for taxis

Staying somewhere

Hotel (booking)

It is best to book accommodation in advance, particularly during high season in the more popular resorts. Most hotels and B&Bs can be booked online. If you do get stuck for a place to stay, a branch of the Greek Tourist Organisation (or Cyprus Tourism Organisation in Cyprus) may be able to help.

FACE TO FACE

Θα ήθελα ένα δίκλινο/μονόκλινο δωμάτιο
tha **ee**thela **e**na dh**ee**kleeno/mon**o**kleeno dhom**a**teeo
I'd like a double/single room

Για πόσα βράδια;
ya p**o**sa vr**a**dheea?
For how many nights?

Για ένα βράδυ/...βράδια
ya **e**na vr**a**dhee/...vr**a**dheea
for one night/...nights

ξενοδοχείο ksenodhokh**ee**o	hotel
δωμάτια dhom**a**teea	rooms (often in private houses)

Do you have any vacancies? — **Έχετε ελεύθερα δωμάτια;**
ekhete el**e**fthera dhom**a**teea?

for tonight — **για απόψε;**
ya ap**o**pse?

We'd like to stay ... nights — **Θα θέλαμε να μείνουμε ... βράδια**
tha th**e**lame na m**ee**noome ... vr**a**dheea

Do you have any bedrooms on the ground floor? — **Έχετε υπνοδωμάτια στο ισόγειο;**
ekhete eepnodhom**a**teea sto ees**o**yeeo?

How much is it per day/ per week? — **Πόσο κοστίζει για μια μέρα/μια βδομάδα;**
p**o**so kost**ee**zee ya mya m**e**ra/ mya vdom**a**da?

for three people — **τρίκλινο**
tr**ee**kleeno

with bath — **με μπάνιο**
me b**a**nyo

with shower — **με ντους**
me doos

with a double bed	**με διπλό κρεβάτι** me dheeplo krevatee
with twin beds	**με δύο κρεβάτια** me dheeo krevatya
a cot	**ένα παιδικό κρεβάτι** ena pedheeko krevatee
A room looking onto the sea	**Ένα δωμάτιο που να βλέπει στη θάλασσα** ena dhomateeo poo na vlepee stee thalasa
How much is it...?	**Πόσο κοστίζει...;** poso kosteezee...?
per night	**το βράδυ** to vradhee
per week	**τη βδομάδα** tee vdhomadha
for half board	**με ημιδιατροφή** me eemeedheeatrofee
for full board	**με πλήρη διατροφή** me pleeree dheeatrofee
Is breakfast included?	**Το πρωινό περιλαμβάνεται στην τιμή;** to proeeno pereelamvanete steen teemee?

YOU MAY HEAR...

| **Είμαστε γεμάτοι**
eemaste yematee | We're full |

54

Hotel desk

. . . .

I booked a room...	**Έκλεισα ένα δωμάτιο...** **e**kleesa **e**na dhom**a**teeo...
by phone	**από το τηλέφωνο** apo to teel**e**fono
in the name of...	**στο όνομα...** sto **o**noma...
I'd like to see the room	**Θα ήθελα να δω το δωμάτιο** tha **ee**thela na dho to dhom**a**teeo
Where is the lift?	**Πού είναι το ασανσέρ;** poo **ee**ne to asans**e**r?
What time is...?	**Τι ώρα σερβίρεται...;** tee **o**ra serv**ee**rete...?
dinner	**το δείπνο** to dh**ee**pno
breakfast	**το πρωινό** to proeen**o**
I reserved the room(s) online	**Κράτησα (έκλεισα) δωμάτιο(-ια) μέσω διαδικτύου** kr**a**teesa (**e**kleesa) dhom**a**t-eeo (-eea) m**e**so dheeadheekt**ee**oo
Does the price include breakfast?	**Στην τιμή συμπεριλαμβάνεται το πρωινό;** steen teem**ee** seempereelamv**a**nete to proeen**o**?

55

Is there a hotel restaurant/bar?	**Υπάρχει εστιατόριο/μπαρ στο ξενοδοχείο;** eep**a**rkhee esteeat**o**reeo/bar sto ksenodokh**ee**o?
The key, please	**Το κλειδί, παρακαλώ** to kleedh**ee**, parakal**o**
room number...	**αριθμός δωματίου...** areethm**o**s dhomat**ee**oo...
Can you keep it in the safe, please?	**Μπορείτε να το φυλάξετε στο χρηματοκιβώτιο;** bor**ee**te na to feel**a**ksete sto khreematokeev**o**teeo?
I'm leaving tomorrow	**Φεύγω αύριο** f**e**vgho **a**vreeo
Are there any toilets for disabled people?	**Υπάρχουν τουαλέτες για άτομα με ειδικές ανάγκες;** eep**a**rkhoon tooal**e**tes ya **a**toma me eedheek**e**s an**a**nges?
Can I leave my luggage until...?	**Μπορώ να αφήσω τις βαλίτσες μου μέχρι...;** bor**o** na af**ee**so tees val**ee**tses moo m**e**khree...?
Please bring me...	**Παρακαλώ φέρτε μου...** parakal**o** f**e**rte moo...
a glass	**ένα ποτήρι** **e**na pot**ee**ree
clean towels	**καθαρές πετσέτες** kathar**e**s pets**e**tes
toilet paper	**χαρτί υγείας** khart**ee** eey**ee**as

56

Camping

● ● ● ● ● ● ● ● ● ● ● ● ● ● ● ● ● ● ●

Although camping is not as popular as in some other European countries, Greece has a number of campsites operated by the Greek Tourist Organisation. The Panhellenic Camping Association's website (**www.greececamping.gr**) provides useful information about camping sites and maps in Greece. There are six campsites in Cyprus. In both countries camping is only permitted on official sites, unauthorised camping can incur hefty fines.

Is there a restaurant on the campsite?	**Υπάρχει εστιατόριο στο κάμπινγκ;** ee**pa**rkhee esteeat**o**reeo sto c**a**mping?
Do you have any vacancies?	**Έχετε ελεύθερες θέσεις;** **e**khete el**e**ftheres th**e**sees?
Are showers.../ Is hot water.../ Is electricity...	**Οι ντουσιέρες.../το ζεστό νερό.../το ηλεκτρικό...** ee doosy**e**res.../to zest**o** ner**o**.../ to eelektreek**o**...
...included in the price?	**...περιλαμβάνονται στην τιμή;** ...pereelamv**a**nonde steen teem**ee**?
We'd like to stay for ... nights	**Θέλουμε να μείνουμε ... βράδια** th**e**loome na m**ee**noome ... vr**a**dheea

How much is it per night...?	**Πόσο κοστίζει τη βραδιά...;**
	p**o**so kost**ee**zee tee vradhee**a**...?
for a tent	**η σκηνή**
	ee skeen**ee**
per person	**το άτομο**
	to **a**tomo

Self-catering

Who do we contact if there are problems?	**Σε ποιον θ' απευθυνθούμε αν υπάρξουν προβλήματα;**
	se py**o**n th-apeftheenth**oo**me an eep**a**rksoon provl**ee**mata?
How does the heating work?	**Πώς λειτουργεί η θέρμανση;**
	pos leetoory**ee** ee th**e**rmansee?
Is there always hot water?	**Έχει πάντα ζεστό νερό;**
	ekhee p**a**nta zest**o** ner**o**?
Where is the nearest supermarket?	**Πού είναι το κοντινότερο σουπερμάρκετ;**
	poo **ee**ne to kondeen**o**tero supermarket?
Where do we leave the rubbish?	**Πού πετάμε τα σκουπίδια;**
	poo pet**a**me ta skoop**ee**dhya?
recycling	**η ανακύκλωση**
	ee anak**ee**klosee

Shopping

Shopping phrases

ταμείο tam**ee**o	cash desk
εδώ πληρώνετε edh**o** pleer**o**nete	pay here

FACE TO FACE

Τι θα θέλατε;
tee tha th**e**late?
What would you like?

Έχετε...;
ekhete...?
Do you have...?

Ναι, φυσικά. Θα θέλατε τίποτε άλλο;
ne, feeseek**a**. Tha th**e**late t**ee**pote **a**llo?
Yes, certainly. Would you like anything else?

Where is...?	**Πού είναι...;** poo **ee**ne...?
Do you sell...?	**Πουλάτε...;** pool**a**te...?

59

Where can I buy...?	**Πού μπορώ να αγοράσω...;** poo bor**o** na aghor**a**so...?
toys	**παιχνίδια** pekhn**ee**dhya
gifts	**δώρα** dh**o**ra
It's too expensive	**Είναι πολύ ακριβό** **ee**ne pol**ee** akreev**o**
Have you anything else?	**Έχετε τίποτε άλλο;** **e**khete t**ee**pote **a**lo?

Shops

baker's	**αρτοποιείο**	artopee-**ee**o
bookshop	**βιβλιοπωλείο**	veevleeopol**ee**o
butcher's	**κρεοπωλείο**	kreopol**ee**o
cake shop	**ζαχαροπλαστείο**	zakharoplast**ee**o
clothes	**ρούχα**	r**oo**kha
gifts	**δώρα**	dh**o**ra
grocer's	**παντοπωλείο**	pantopol**ee**o
hairdresser's	**κομμωτήριο**	komoteer**ee**o
pharmacy	**φαρμακείο**	farmak**ee**o
shoe shop	**κατάστημα υποδημάτων**	kat**a**steema eepodheem**a**ton
shop	**κατάστημα**	kat**a**steema

souvenir shop	κατάστημα αναμνηστικών ειδών	katasteema anamneesteekon eedon
stationer's	χαρτοπωλείο	khartopoleeo
supermarket	σουπερμάρκετ	supermarket
toy shop	παιχνίδια	pekhneedheea

Food (general)

. . . .

biscuits	τα μπισκότα	beeskota
bread	το ψωμί	psomee
butter	το βούτυρο	vooteero
cheese	το τυρί	teeree
chicken	το κοτόπουλο	kotopoolo
coffee (instant)	το Νεσκαφέ®	nescafe
crisps	τα πατατάκια	patatakya
eggs	τα αβγά	avgha
ham	το ζαμπόν	zambon
honey	το μέλι	melee
jam	η μαρμελάδα	marmeladha
marmalade	η μαρμελάδα πορτοκάλι	marmeladha portokalee
milk	το γάλα	ghala
olive oil	το ελαιόλαδο	eleoladho

orange juice	ο χυμός πορτοκαλιού	kheemos portokalyoo
pepper	το πιπέρι	peeperee
salt	το αλάτι	alatee
sugar	η ζάχαρη	zakharee
tea	το τσάι	tsaee
vinegar	το ξύδι	kseedhee
yoghurt	το γιαούρτι	yaoortee

Food (fruit and veg)

Fruit

apples	τα μήλα	meela
apricots	τα βερίκοκα	vereekoka
bananas	οι μπανάνες	bananes
cherries	τα κεράσια	kerasya
figs	τα σύκα	seeka
grapefruit	τα γκρέιπφρουτ	grapefruit
grapes	τα σταφύλια	stafeelya
lemon	το λεμόνι	lemonee
melon	το πεπόνι	peponee
oranges	τα πορτοκάλια	portokalya
peaches	τα ροδάκινα	rodhakeena

pears	τα αχλάδια	akhladhya
strawberries	οι φράουλες	fraooles
watermelon	το καρπούζι	karpoozee

Vegetables

asparagus	τα σπαράγγια	sparanghya
carrots	τα καρότα	karota
cauliflower	το κουνουπίδι	koonoopeedhee
courgettes	τα κολοκυθάκια	kolokeethakya
cucumber	το αγγούρι	angooree
garlic	το σκόρδο	skordho
lettuce	το μαρούλι	maroolee
mushrooms	τα μανιτάρια	maneetarya
onions	τα κρεμμύδια	kremeedhya
peas	ο αρακάς	arakas
peppers	οι πιπεριές	peeperyes
potatoes	οι πατάτες	patates
spinach	το σπανάκι	spanakee
tomatoes	οι ντομάτες	domates

Clothes

• •

The Greek for 'size' is **νούμερο** (n**oo**mero).

women's sizes		men's suit sizes		shoe sizes			
UK	EU	UK	EU	UK	EU	UK	EU
8	36	36	46	2	35	7	40
10	38	38	48	3	36	8	41
12	40	40	50	4	37	9	42
14	42	42	52	5	38	10	43
16	44	44	54	6	39	11	44
18	46	46	56				

FACE TO FACE

Μπορώ να το δοκιμάσω;
bor**o** na to dhokeem**a**so?
May I try this on?

Ναι, φυσικά
ne, feeseek**a**
Yes, of course

Έχετε μεγαλύτερο/μικρότερο νούμερο;
ekhete meghal**ee**tero/meekr**o**tero n**oo**mero?
Do you have a larger/smaller size?

Τι νούμερο φοράτε;
tee n**oo**mero for**a**te?
What size do you take?

Where are the changing rooms?	**Πού είναι τα δοκιμαστήρια;** poo **ee**ne ta dhokeemast**ee**reea?
Do you have this...?	**Έχετε αυτό...;** **e**khete aft**o**...?
in my size	**στο νούμερό μου** sto n**oo**mero moo
in other colours	**σε άλλα χρώματα** se **a**la khr**o**mata
I'm just looking	**Απλώς κοιτάζω** apl**o**s keet**a**zo
I'll take it	**Θα το πάρω** tha to p**a**ro

Clothes (articles)

. . . .

coat	**το παλτό**	palt**o**
dress	**το φόρεμα**	f**o**rema
jacket	**η ζακέτα**	zak**e**ta
pyjamas	**οι πυτζάμες**	peetz**a**mes
shirt	**το πουκάμισο**	pook**a**meeso

65

shorts	το σορτς	sorts
skirt	η φούστα	foosta
socks	οι κάλτσες	kaltses
suit	το κοστούμι	kostoomee
swimsuit	το μαγιό	mayo
top	η μπλούζα	blooza
trousers	το παντελόνι	pandelonee
t-shirt	το μπλουζάκι	bloozakee

Maps and guides

Have you...?	Έχετε...;	ekhete...?
a map of the town	έναν χάρτη της πόλης	enan khartee tees polees
Can you show me (name of place) on the map?	Μπορείτε να μου δείξετε ... πάνω στο χάρτη;	boreete na moo dheeksete ... pano sto khartee?
Do you have...?	Έχετε...;	ekhete...?
a guide book	έναν οδηγό	enan odheegho
in English	στα αγγλικά	sta angleeka

Post office

• •

Opening hours of post offices in Greece vary from place to place and according to the time of year. However, most of them close at midday, apart from those in major cities.

ταχυδρομείο takheedhrom**ee**o	post office
γραμματόσημα ghramat**o**seema	stamps

Do you sell stamps?	**Πουλάτε γραμματόσημα;** pool**a**te ghramat**o**seema?
Is there a post office near here?	**Υπάρχει ταχυδρομείο εδώ κοντά;** eep**a**rkhee takheedhrom**ee**o edh**o** kond**a**?
Stamps for postcards to Great Britain	**Γραμματόσημα για κάρτες για τη Μεγάλη Βρετανία** ghramat**o**seema ya k**a**rtes ya tee megh**a**lee vretan**ee**a

Technology

• • • • • • • • • • • • • • • • • •

Κάρτα μνήμης Karta mn**ee**mees	memory card
εκτυπώνω ekteep**o**no	to print
η ψηφιακή κάμερα psefeeak**ee** c**a**mera	digital camera
το ηλεκτρονικό τσιγάρο to eelektroneek**o** tseegh**a**ro	e-cigarette

Do you have batteries for this camera? | **Έχετε μπαταρίες γι'αυτήν τη φωτογραφική μηχανή;**
ekhete batar**ee**-es yaft**ee**n tee fotoghrafeek**ee** meekhan**ee**?

Can you repair...? | **Μπορείτε να επισκευάσετε...;**
bor**ee**te na epeeskev**a**sete...?

my screen | **την οθόνη** teen oth**o**nee

my keypad | **το πληκτρολόγιο**
to pleektrol**o**gheeo

my charger | **τον φορτιστή μου**
ton forteest**ee** moo

I want to print my photos | **Θέλω να εκτυπώσω τις φωτογραφίες μου**
th**e**lo na ekteep**o**so tees fotoghraf**ee**es moo

I have it on my USB	**Το έχω στο στικάκι/USB μου**
	to **e**kho sto steek**a**kee moo/USB moo
It have it on my e-mail	**Το έχω στα email μου**
	to **e**kho sta email moo

Leisure

Sightseeing and tourist office

. . . .

The Greek Tourist Organisation (**EOT**) has offices
in the larger towns in Greece, as does the Cyprus
Tourism Organisation (**KOT**) in Cyprus. If you are
looking for somewhere to stay, they should have
details of hotels and campsites as well as of
transport, local sights and events.

Where is the tourist office?	**Πού είναι το τουριστικό γραφείο;** poo **ee**ne to tooreesteek**o** ghraf**ee**o?
What can we visit in the area?	**Τι μπορούμε να δούμε σ' αυτήν την περιοχή;** tee bor**oo**me na dh**oo**me saft**ee**n teen pereeokh**ee**?
When can we visit...?	**Πότε μπορούμε να επισκεφθούμε...;** p**o**te bor**oo**me na epeeskefth**oo**me...?
the church	**την εκκλησία** teen eklees**ee**a

| the museum | **το μουσείο** |
| | to moos**ee**o |

| Are there any excursions? | **Γίνονται εκδρομές;** |
| | y**ee**nonte ekdhrom**e**s? |

| Is it ok to bring children? | **Υπάρχει πρόβλημα αν φέρουμε τα παιδιά;** |
| | eep**a**rkhee pr**o**vleema an f**e**roome ta pedhy**a**? |

| How much does the entrance cost? | **Πόσο κάνει η είσοδος;** |
| | p**o**so k**a**nee ee **ee**sodhos? |

| Are there any reductions for...? | **Γίνεται έκπτωση για...;** |
| | y**ee**nete **e**kptosee ya...? |

| students | **φοιτητές** |
| | feeteet**e**s |

| senior citizens | **ηλικιωμένους** |
| | eeleekeeom**e**noos |

When sightseeing, you'll find churches and little chapels everywhere, even in the remotest areas. Greece is an Orthodox Christian country. Sunday services and major religious celebrations, such as Easter, are very popular. Do not be surprised to see road shrines, people making the sign of the cross, or people spitting and saying 'ftou-ftou' to protect themselves from the evil eye.

Entertainment

• •

Details of entertainments can be found in newspapers. Tourist offices will also have information on local festivals. There are two major English language newspapers in Greece, **KATHIMERINI** and **ATHENS NEWS**, both of which include listings for cinemas, general entertainment and events.

What is there to do in the evenings?	**Τι μπορεί να κάνει κανείς τα βράδια;** tee bor**ee** na k**a**nee kan**ee**s ta vr**a**dheea?
Is there anything for children?	**Υπάρχει τίποτε για παιδιά;** eep**a**rkhee t**ee**pote ya pedhy**a**?

YOU MAY HEAR...

Η είσοδος περιλαμβάνει και ένα ποτό ee **ee**sodhos pereelamv**a**nee ke **e**na pot**o**	The entry fee includes one free drink

Nightlife

• •

Where can I go clubbing?	**Πού θα μπορούσα να πάω για κλάμπινγκ;** poo tha bor**oo**sa na p**a**o ya clubbing?

το νυχτερινό κλάμπ to neekhtereen**o** club	nightclub
Φεστιβάλ Μουσικής festival mooseek**ee**s	music festival
η παμπ ee pub	pub
το μπαρ to bar	bar
η συναυλία/παράσταση ee seenavl**ee**a/par**a**stasee	gig
το πάρτυ to party	party
το γκέι μπαρ/κλάμπ to gay bar/club	gay bar/club

Religious beliefs still play an important role in shaping public opinion. Homosexuality is not tolerated by the Greek Orthodox Church. Nevertheless, Athens and many tourist destinations are very welcoming to gay and lesbian travellers.

Out and about

• • • • • • • • • • • • • • • • •

Where can I go...?	**Πού μπορώ να πάω για...;** poo bor**o** na p**a**o ya...?
fishing	**ψάρεμα** ps**a**rema
Is there a swimming pool?	**Υπάρχει πισίνα;** eep**a**rkhee pees**ee**na?
When can we hire bikes?	**Πότε μπορούμε να νοικιάσουμε ποδήλατα;** p**o**te bor**oo**me na neeky**a**soome podh**ee**lata?
How much is it...?	**Πόσο κοστίζει...;** p**o**so kost**ee**zee...?
per hour	**την ώρα** teen **o**ra
per day	**τη μέρα** tee m**e**ra
Can you visit ... in a wheelchair?	**Μπορεί κανείς να επισκεφτεί ... με καρότσι;** bor**ee** kan**ee**s na epeeskeft**ee** ... me kar**o**tsee?

During summer, on Saints' days, villages on the mainland and on the islands run local festivals called **πανηγύρια** (paneey**ee**reea) with food and music. Another unmissable event is the August Full Moon Festival. Many of the best archaeological sites are open for free until late. The festival is also accompanied by performances of theatre, music and dance.

What's on at the theatre?	**Τι παίζει το θέατρο;** tee p**e**zee to th**e**atro?
Two tickets...	**Δύο εισιτήρια...** dh**ee**o eeseet**ee**reea...
for tonight	**για απόψε** ya ap**o**pse
for tomorrow night	**για αύριο βράδυ** ya **a**vreeo vr**a**dhee

Classical Greek plays are famously performed at the theatre of *Herod Atticus* at the foot of the Acropolis in Athens, and at the theatre at Epidavros in the Peloponnese. An English translation of the play would help if you aren't familiar with the plot. Tip: ancient theatres have stone seats so it may be a good idea to take a cushion!

adventure centre	**κέντρο αναψυχής**	k**e**ntro anapseekh**ee**s
art gallery	**η γκαλερί/ αίθουσα τέχνης**	gallery/ **e**thoosa t**e**khnees
boat hire	**ενοικίαση σκαφών**	eneek**ee**asee skaf**o**n
camping	**η κατασκήνωση**	katask**ee**nosee
museum	**το μουσείο**	moos**ee**o

piercing	**το τρύπημα**	tr**ee**peema
tattoo	**το τατουάζ**	tatoo**az**
theme park	**το λούνα παρκ**	luna park
water park	**το θαλάσιο πάρκο**	thal**a**seeo p**a**rko
zoo	**ο ζωολογικός κήπος**	zo-ologheek**os** k**ee**pos

Music

. . . .

| Are there any good concerts on? | **Υπάρχει καμία καλή συναυλία;** eep**a**rkhee kam**ee**a kal**ee** seenavl**ee**a? |
| Where can I hear some Greek music and songs? | **Πού μπορώ να ακούσω ελληνική μουσική και τραγούδια;** poo bor**o** na ak**oo**so eleeneek**ee** mooseek**ee** ke tragh**oo**dhya? |

folk	**η παραδοσιακή μουσική**	paradhoseeak**ee** mooseek**ee**
hip-hop	**η χιπ-χοπ**	kheep-khop
pop	**η ποπ**	pop
reggae	**η ρέγκε**	r**e**ge
rock	**η ροκ**	rok
techno	**η τέκνο**	tekno

Beach

● ●

Is there a good beach near here?	**Υπάρχει μία καλή παραλία εδώ κοντά;** eep**a**rkhee m**ee**a kal**ee** paral**ee**a edh**o** kond**a**?
Can I get there...?	**Μπορώ να πάω εκεί...;** bor**o** na p**a**o ek**ee**...?
by bus	**με λεωφορείο** me leofor**ee**o
by car	**με αυτοκίνητο** me aftok**ee**neeto
Can I hire...?	**Μπορώ να νοικιάσω...;** bor**o** na neeky**a**so...?
a deckchair	**μια ξαπλώστρα** mya ksapl**o**stra
an umbrella	**μια ομπρέλα** mya ombr**e**la

YOU MAY HEAR...

Απαγορεύεται το κολύμπι Apaghor**e**vete to kol**ee**bee	No swimming
Απαγορεύονται οι βουτιές Apaghor**e**vonte ee vootee**e**s	No diving

Sport

Leisure

Where can I...?	**Πού μπορώ να...;**
	poo bor**o** na...?
play tennis	**παίξω τένις**
	p**e**kso t**e**nees
go swimming	**κολυμπήσω**
	koleemb**ee**so
go jogging	**κάνω τζόκινγκ**
	k**a**no j**o**gging
go for a walk	**κάνω μία βόλτα**
	k**a**no m**ee**a v**o**lta
I want to try...	**Θέλω να δοκιμάσω...**
	th**e**lo na dhokeem**a**so...
I've never done this before	**Δεν το έχω δοκιμάσει ποτέ**
	dhen to **e**kho dhokeem**a**see pot**e**
Can I hire...?	**Μπορώ να νοικιάσω...;**
	bor**o** na neeky**a**so...?
rackets	**ρακέτες**
	rak**e**tes
How many kilometres is the walk?	**Πόσα χιλιόμετρα είναι ο περίπατος;**
	p**o**sa kheely**o**metra **ee**ne o per**ee**patos?
We'd like to go mountain climbing	**Θα θέλαμε να κάνουμε ορειβασία**
	tha th**e**lame na k**a**noome oreevas**ee**a

78

cycling	η ποδηλασία	podheelas**ee**a
dancing	ο χορός	khor**o**s
kayaking	το καγιάκ	k**a**yak
rock climbing	η αναρρίχηση	anarr**ee**kheesee
snowboarding	η χιονοσανίδα (σνόουμπορντ)	khionosan**ee**dha
volleyball	το βόλεϊ	volley
water-skiing	το θαλάσσιο σκι	thal**a**seeo sk**ee**
windsurfing	η ιστιοσανίδα (γουίντ σέρφινγκ)	eesteeosan**ee**dha

Telephone and mobile

· ·

To phone Greece from the UK, the international code is **oo 30** followed by the Greek area code and the phone number you require. For Cyprus, dial **oo 357** followed by the Cyprus area code and the phone number.

FACE TO FACE

Παρακαλώ/Ναι
parakal**o**/ne
Hello

Θα ήθελα να μιλήσω στον/στην...
tha **ee**thela na meel**ee**so ston/steen...
I'd like to speak to...

Ποιος είστε;
py**o**s **ee**ste?
Who's calling?

Είμαι η Μαρία
eeme ee Mar**i**a
It's Maria

Ένα λεπτό.../Περιμένετε, παρακαλώ
ena lept**o**.../pereem**e**nete, parakal**o**
Just a moment.../Hold on, please

I want to make a phone call	**Θέλω να κάνω ένα τηλεφώνημα** thelo na kano ena teelefoneema
What is your mobile number?	**Ποιός είναι ο αριθμός του κινητού σας (τηλεφώνου);** pyos eene o areethmos too keenetoo sas (teelefonoo)?
My mobile number is...	**Ο αριθμός του κινητού μου (τηλεφώνου) είναι…** o areethmos too keenetoo moo (teelefonoo) eene...
Can I borrow your...?	**Μπορώ να δανειστώ το/τη …σου;** boro na dhaneesto to/tee...?
smartphone	**το έξυπνο τηλέφωνο** to ekseepno teelefono
charger	**ο φορτιστής** o forteestees
Do you have a ... charger/cable?	**Έχετε φορτιστή/καλώδιο για…;** ekhete forteestee/kalodheeo ya...?
I have an e-ticket on my phone	**Έχω ένα ηλεκτρονικό εισητήριο στο κινητό μου** ekho ena eelektroneeko eeseeteereeo sto keeneeto moo
I need to phone a UK/US/ an Australian number	**Χρειάζεται να καλέσω έναν τηλεφωνικό αριθμό στη(ν) Βρετανία/Αμερική/ Αυστραλία** khreeazete na kaleso enan teelefoneeko areethmo stee(n) vretaneea/amereekee/ afstraleea

Πήρατε λάθος αριθμό p**ee**rate l**a**thos areethm**o**	You've got the wrong number
Παρακαλούμε να κλείσετε τα κινητά τηλέφωνα parakal**oo**me na kl**ee**sete ta keeneet**a** teel**e**fona	Please switch off all mobiles

Text messaging

· ·

Although there are some abbreviated expressions in Greek used for texting and social media, note that Greek people regularly use the most popular text messaging terms in English too.

μνμ	**Μήνυμα**	text
φλκ	**Φιλάκια**	kisses
τπτ	**Τίποτα**	nothing
τλμ	**Τα λέμε**	talk to you soon/ see you later
τεσπα	**Τέλος πάντων**	anyway
σκ/ΣΚ	**Σαββατοκύριακο**	weekend

text (message)	**το μήνυμα** to m**ee**neema
to send a text (message)	**στέλνω μήνυμα** st**e**lno m**ee**neema

E-mail

• •

Although you will hear the English word e-mail
used, the proper Greek term for e-mail address
is **η ηλεκτρονική διεύθυνση** (ee eelektroneek**ee**
dhee-**e**ftheensee).

Do you have e-mail?	**Έχετε e-mail;** **e**khete e-mail?
My e-mail address is...	**Η διεύθυνση e-mail μου** **είναι...** ee dhee-**e**fthensee e-mail moo **ee**ne...

Internet

• •

app	**η εφαρμογή** ee efarmogh**ee**
laptop	**ο φορητός υπολογιστής** o foreet**o**s eepologheest**ee**s

social network	**η κοινωνική δικτύωση**
	ee keenoneek**ee** dheekt**ee**osee
tablet	**η ταμπλέτα**
	tabl**e**ta
Wi-Fi	**η ασύρματη σύνδεση**
	ee as**ee**rmatee s**ee**ndhesee
What is the Wi-Fi password?	**Ποιος είναι ο κωδικός πρόσβασης;**
	py**o**s **ee**ne o kodhik**o**s pr**o**svasees?
Do you have free Wi-Fi?	**Έχετε δωρεάν ασύρματη σύνδεση;**
	ekhete dore**a**n as**ee**rmatee s**ee**ndhesee wi-fi?
Add me on Facebook	**Βάλε με στο Facebook**
	v**a**lee me sto Facebook
Is there a 3G/4G signal?	**Υπάρχει σήμα 3G/4G;**
	eep**a**rkhei s**ee**ma 3G/4G?
I need to access my webmail	**Χρειάζομαι πρόσβαση στην ηλεκτρονική μου αλληλογραφία**
	khree**a**zome pr**o**svasee steen eelektroneek**ee** moo alleeloghraf**ee**a
I would like to use Skype	**Θα ήθελα να χρησιμοποιήσω το Skype**
	tha **ee**thela na khreeseemopee-**ee**so to Skype

Practicalities

Money

· ·

Banks in Greece and Cyprus are generally open during the morning.

Greece 8.30 a.m. to 2.30 p.m. Monday to Thursday, 8 a.m. to 2 p.m. on Fridays.

Cyprus 8.15 a.m. to 1.30 p.m. Monday to Friday from May to September, but 8.30 a.m. to 1.30 p.m. from October to April.

τράπεζα tra**p**eza	bank
πιστωτικές κάρτες peestoteek**e**s k**a**rtes	credit cards
δολλάρια dholl**a**reea	dollars
λίρες αγγλίας l**ee**res angl**ee**as	pounds
η τιμή συναλλάγματος ee teem**ee** seenal**a**ghmatos	exchange rate

Where can I change some money?	**Πού μπορώ να αλλάξω χρήματα;** poo boro na alakso khreemata?
Where is the nearest bank?	**Πού είναι η κοντινότερη τράπεζα;** poo eene ee kondeenoteree trapeza?
What is the exchange rate for...?	**Ποια είναι η τιμή συναλλάγματος για...;** pya eene ee teemee seenalaghamatos ya...?
When does the bank close?	**Πότε κλείνει η τράπεζα;** pote kleenee ee trapeza?

Paying

• •

ευρώ evro	euro
λεπτά lepta	cents
λογαριασμός loghareeasmos	bill
ταμείο tameeo	cash desk
τιμολόγιο teemoloyeeo	invoice
απόδειξη apodheeksee	receipt
μόνο μετρητά mono metreeta	cash only

να βγάλω χρήματα από την τράπεζα na vgh**a**lo khr**ee**mata apo teen tr**a**peza	to withdraw money
η χρεωστική κάρτα ee khreosteek**ee** k**a**rta	debit card
η πιστωτική κάρτα ee peestoteek**ee** k**a**rta	credit card
ανέπαφη πληρωμή an**e**pafee pleerom**ee**	contactless payment
η προπληρωμένη κάρτα συναλλάγματος ee propleerom**e**ni karta seenal**a**ghmatos	prepaid currency card

How much is it?	**Πόσο κάνει;** p**o**so k**a**nee?
Do you take credit cards?	**Παίρνετε πιστωτικές κάρτες;** p**e**rnete peestoteek**e**s k**a**rtes?
I need a receipt	**Χρειάζομαι απόδειξη** khree**a**zome ap**o**dheeksee
Where do I pay?	**Πού πληρώνω;** poo pleer**o**no?
Can I pay in cash?	**Μπορώ να πληρώσω σε μετρητά;** boro na pleer**o**so se metreet**a?**

Where is the nearest cash machine?	**Πού είναι το κοντινότερο μηχάνημα ανάληψης χρημάτων;** poo **ee**ne to konteen**o**tero meekh**a**neema an**a**leepsees khreem**a**ton?
Is there a credit card charge?	**Υπάρχει επιβάρυνση στην πιστωτική κάρτα;** eep**a**rkhee epeev**a**reensee steen peestoteek**ee** k**a**rta?
Is there a discount for senior citizens?	**Κάνετε έκπτωση σε συνταξιούχους;** k**a**nete **e**kptosee se seentaksee**oo**khoos?
Is there a reduction for children?	**Υπάρχει ειδική τιμή για παιδιά;** eep**a**rkhee eedheek**ee** teem**ee** ya pedhy**a**?
Can you write down the price?	**Μπορείτε να μου γράψετε την τιμή;** bor**ee**te na moo gr**a**psete teen teem**ee**?

Luggage

• •

| My luggage hasn't arrived | **Οι αποσκευές μου δεν έφτασαν** ee aposkev**e**s moo dhen **e**ftasan |

88

My suitcase has arrived damaged	**Η βαλίτσα μου έφτασε χαλασμένη**
	ee val**ee**tsa moo **e**ftase khalasm**e**nee
Can I leave my luggage here?	**Μπορώ να αφήσω εδώ τις αποσκευές μου;**
	bor**o** na af**ee**so edh**o** tees aposkev**e**s moo?

YOU MAY HEAR...

| **Μπορείτε να τις αφήσετε εδώ μέχρι τις 6 η ώρα** bor**ee**te na tees af**ee**sete edh**o** m**e**khree tees **e**ksee ee **o**ra | You may leave it here until 6 o'clock |

Repairs

This is broken	**Έσπασε αυτό**
	espase aft**o**
Where can I get this repaired?	**Πού θα μου το επισκευάσουν;**
	poo tha moo to epeeskev**a**soon?
Is it worth repairing?	**Αξίζει τον κόπο να επισκευαστεί;**
	aks**ee**zee ton k**o**po na epeeskevast**ee**?

Laundry

Where can I do some washing?	**Πού μπορώ να πλύνω μερικά ρούχα;** poo boro na pleeno mereeka rookha?
Is there a dry-cleaner's near here?	**Υπάρχει καθαριστήριο εδώ κοντά;** eeparkhee kathareesteereeo edho konda?

Complaints

The ... doesn't work	**ο/η/το ... δε δουλεύει** o/ee/to ... dhe dhooleevee
The ... don't work	**οι/τα ... δε δουλεύουν** ee/ta ... dhe dhoolevoon
lights	**τα φώτα** ta fota
heating	**η θέρμανση** ee thermansee
air conditioning	**ο κλιματισμός** o kleemateesmos
This is dirty	**Αυτό είναι βρόμικο** afto eene vromeeko

There's a problem with the room	**Υπάρχει πρόβλημα με το δωμάτιο** eep**a**rkhee pr**o**vleema me to dhom**a**teeo
It's noisy	**Έχει θόρυβο** **e**khee th**o**reevo
I want a refund	**Θέλω τα χρήματά μου πίσω** th**e**lo ta khr**ee**mat**a** moo p**ee**so

Problems

Can you help me?	**Μπορείτε να με βοηθήσετε;** bor**ee**te na me voeeth**ee**sete?
I only speak a little Greek	**Μιλάω μόνο λίγα ελληνικά** meel**a**o m**o**no l**ee**gha eleeneek**a**
Does anyone here speak English?	**Μιλά κανείς εδώ αγγλικά;** meel**a** kan**ee**s edh**o** angleek**a**?
I would like to speak to whoever is in charge	**Θα ήθελα να μιλήσω στον υπεύθυνο** tha **ee**thela na meel**ee**so ston eep**e**ftheeno
I'm lost	**Έχω χαθεί** **e**kho khath**ee**
How do I get to...?	**Πώς θα πάω στο...;** p**o**s tha p**a**o sto...?

I've missed...	**Έχασα...** **e**khasa...
my bus	**το λεωφορείο μου** to leofor**ee**o moo
my plane	**το αεροπλάνο μου** to aeropl**a**no moo
Can you show me how this works?	**Μπορείτε να μου δείξετε πώς δουλεύει αυτό;** bor**ee**te na moo dh**ee**ksete pos dhool**e**vee aft**o**?
I have lost my purse	**Έχασα το πορτοφόλι μου** **e**khasa to portof**o**lee moo
I need to get to...	**Πρέπει να φτάσω στο...** pr**e**pee na ft**a**so sto...
Where can I recycle this?	**Πού μπορώ να το ανακυκλώσω αυτό;** poo bor**o** na to anakeekl**o**so aft**o**?
I need to access my online banking	**Χρειάζομαι πρόσβαση στον ηλεκτρονικό τραπεζικό λογαριασμό μου** khree**a**zome pr**o**svasee ston eelektroneek**o** trapezeek**o** loghariasm**o** moo
Do you have wheelchairs?	**Έχετε καρότσια;** **e**khete kar**o**tsya?

Emergencies

· ·

The emergency numbers in Greece (for Athens) are police 100, ambulance 166, fire 199 and tourist police 171. In Cyprus the emergency number for all these services is 199.

αστυνομία asteenom**ee**a	police
ασθενοφόρο asthenof**o**ro	ambulance
πυροσβεστική peerosvesteek**ee**	fire brigade

Help!	**Βοήθεια!** vo**ee**theea!
Fire!	**Φωτιά!** foty**a**!
Can you help me?	**Μπορείτε να με βοηθήσετε;** bor**ee**te na me voeeth**ee**sete?
There's been an accident!	**Έγινε ατύχημα!** **e**yeene at**ee**kheema!
Someone is injured	**Κάποιος τραυματίστηκε** k**a**pyos travmat**ee**steeke

Call...	**Φωνάξτε...** fonakste...
the police	**την αστυνομία** teen asteenomeea
an ambulance	**ένα ασθενοφόρο** ena asthenoforo
Where is the police station?	**Πού είναι το αστυνομικό τμήμα;** poo eene to asteenomeeko tmeema?
I've been robbed	**Με έκλεψαν** me eklepsan
I want to report a theft	**Θέλω να αναφέρω μια κλοπή** thelo na anafero mya klopee
My car has been stolen	**Μου έκλεψαν το αυτοκίνητο** moo eklepsan to aftokeeneeto
Someone's stolen my bag	**Κάποιος μου έκλεψε την τσάντα** kapyos moo eklepse teen tsanda
My car has been broken into	**Μου παραβίασαν το αυτοκίνητο** moo paraveeasan to aftokeeneeto
I've been attacked	**Μου επιτέθηκαν** moo epeetetheekan
I've been raped	**Με βίασαν** me veeasan
I want to speak to a policewoman	**Θέλω να μιλήσω σε γυναίκα αστυνομικό** thelo na meeleeso se yeeneka asteenomeeko

94

I need to make an urgent telephone call	**Πρέπει να κάνω ένα επείγον τηλεφώνημα** prepee na kano ena epeeghon teelefoneema
I need a report for my insurance	**Θέλω μια αναφορά για την ασφαλιστική μου εταιρεία** thelo mya anafora ya teen asfaleesteekee moo etereea
How much is the fine?	**Πόσο είναι το πρόστιμο;** poso eene to prosteemo?
Where do I pay it?	**Πού θα το πληρώσω;** poo tha to pleeroso?

YOU MAY HEAR...

Περάσατε με κόκκινο perasate me kokeeno	You went through a red light

Pharmacy

• •

You can consult a pharmacist on minor medical issues or illnesses. There is at least one doctor on every island. Larger islands have public hospitals and private practices.

| **φαρμακείο** farmak**ee**o | pharmacy/chemist |
| **συνταγή** seenday**ee** | prescription |

I don't feel well	**Δεν αισθάνομαι καλά** dhen esth**a**nome kal**a**
Have you something for...?	**Έχετε τίποτε για...;** **e**khete t**ee**pote ya...?
sunburn	**τα εγκαύματα** ta eng**a**vmata
travel sickness	**τη ναυτία** tee naft**ee**a
diarrhoea	**τη διάρροια** tee dhee**a**reea

Is it safe for children?	**Είναι ασφαλές για παιδιά;**	
	eene asfal**e**s ya pedy**a**?	
How much should I give?	**Πόσο πρέπει να δώσω;**	
	p**o**so pr**e**pee na dh**o**so?	

Να το παίρνετε τρεις φορές την ημέρα πριν/ με/μετά το φαγητό na to p**e**rnete trees for**e**s teen eem**e**ra preen/me/ met**a** to fayeet**o**	Take it three times a day before/with/after meals

asthma	**το άσθμα**	**a**sthma
condom	**το προφυλακτικό**	profeelakteek**o**
contact lenses	**οι φακοί επαφής**	fak**ee** epaf**ee**s
inhaler	**η συσκευή εισπνοής**	seeskev**ee** eespno**ee**s
morning-after pill	**το χάπι της επόμενης μέρας**	kh**a**pee tees ep**o**menees m**e**ras
mosquito bite	**το τσίμπημα κουνουπιού**	ts**ee**mbeema koonoopee**oo**
painkillers	**τα παυσίπονα**	pafs**ee**pona
period	**η περίοδος**	per**ee**odhos
the Pill	**το αντισυλληπτικό**	anteeseelleep- teek**o** kh**a**pee
tampon	**το ταμπόν**	tamp**o**n

Health

Doctor

FACE TO FACE

Δεν νιώθω καλά
then neeotho kala
I don't feel very well

Έχετε πυρετό;
ekhete peereto?
Do you have a temperature?

Όχι, πονάω εδώ...
okhi, ponao edho...
No, I have a pain here...

I need a doctor	**Χρειάζομαι γιατρό** khreeazome yatro
My son is ill	**Ο γιος μου είναι άρρωστος** o yos moo eene arostos
My daughter is ill	**Η κόρη μου είναι άρρωστη** ee koree moo eene arostee
I'm pregnant	**Είμαι έγγυος** eeme engeeos
I'm diabetic	**Είμαι διαβητικός(-ή)** eeme dheeaveeteek-os(-ee)
I'm allergic to penicillin	**Έχω αλλεργία στην πενικιλλίνη** ekho aleryeea steen peneekeeleenee

I'm allergic to...	**Είμαι αλλεργικ-ός/ή...**
	eeme aleryeek-**os**/**ee**...
pollen	**στη γύρη** stee gh**ee**ree
dairy	**στα γαλακτοκομικά**
	sta ghalaktokomeek**a**
gluten	**στη γλουτένη** stee gloot**e**nee
nuts	**στους ξηρούς καρπούς**
	stoos kseer**oo**s karpoos
I have a prescription for...	**Έχω μία συνταγή γιατρού για...**
	ekho m**y**a seentagh**ee** yatr**oo** ya...
I've run out of medication	**Μου τελείωσε το φάρμακο**
	moo tel**ee**ose to f**a**rmako
My blood group is...	**Η ομάδα αίματός μου είναι...**
	ee om**a**dha **e**mat**o**s moo **ee**ne...
I've been stung by something	**Κάτι με τσίμπησε**
	k**a**tee me ts**ee**mbeese
I need a receipt for the insurance	**Χρειάζομαι απόδειξη για την ασφαλιστική μου εταιρεία**
	khree**a**zome ap**o**dheeksee ya teen asfaleesteek**ee** moo eter**ee**a
epilepsy	**η επιληψία**
	ee epeeleeps**ee**a

STI or STD (sexually transmitted infection/ disease)	**σεξουαλικά μεταδιδόμενη μόλυνση/μεταδιδόμενο νόσημα** seksooaleeka metadheedhomenee moleensee/metadheedhomeno noseema
food poisoning	**η τροφική δηλητηρίαση** ee trofeekee dheeleeteereeasee
headache	**ο πονοκέφαλος** o ponokefalos
drug abuse	**η κατάχρηση φαρμάκων** ee katakhreesee farmakon
sprain	**το διάστρεμα** to dhiastrema
GP (general practitioner)	**ο παθολόγος/οικογενειακός γιατρός** o pathologhos/eekoyeneeakos yatros
A&E (accident and emergency)	**τα επείγοντα (περιστατικά)** ta epeeghonda (pereestateeka)

Μην πίνετε αλκοόλ meen p**ee**nete alko**ol**	Do not drink alcohol	
Πίνετε; p**ee**nete?	Do you drink?	
Καπνίζετε; kapn**ee**zete?	Do you smoke?	
Παίρνετε φάρμακα; p**e**rnete f**a**rmaka	Do you take drugs?	

arm	**το μπράτσο**	br**a**tso
back	**η πλάτη**	pl**a**tee
chest	**ο θώρακας**	th**o**rakas
ear	**το αυτί**	aft**ee**
eye	**το μάτι**	m**a**tee
foot	**το πέλμα**	p**e**lma
head	**το κεφάλι**	kef**a**lee
heart	**η καρδιά**	kardhee**a**
leg	**το πόδι**	p**o**dhee
neck	**ο λαιμός**	lem**o**s
toe	**το δάχτυλο του ποδιού**	dh**a**khteelo too podhee**oo**
tooth	**το δόντι**	dh**o**ndee
wrist	**ο καρπός**	karp**o**s

Health

Dentist

• • • • • • • • • • • • • • • • • • • •

I need a dentist	**Χρειάζομαι οδοντίατρο** khree**a**zome odhond**ee**atro
He/She has toothache	**Έχει πονόδοντο** **e**khee pon**o**dhondo
Can you do a temporary filling?	**Μπορείτε να κάνετε προσωρινό σφράγισμα;** bor**ee**te na k**a**nete prosoreen**o** sfr**a**-yeesma?
It hurts (me)	**Με πονάει** me pon**a**ee
Can you give me something for the pain?	**Μπορείτε να μου δώσετε κάτι για τον πόνο;** bor**ee**te na moo dh**o**sete k**a**tee ya ton p**o**no?

YOU MAY HEAR...

Πρέπει να βγει pr**e**pee na vyee	It has to come out

Eating out

Eating places

μπαρ (bar) Serves drinks and sometimes snacks.

καφετερία (kafet**e**reea) Serves drinks, coffee, light meals, snacks.

ταβέρνα (tav**e**rna) Either a traditional tavern or an establishment aimed at the tourist.

ουζερί (oozer**ee**) A small bar serving ouzo and other traditional drinks. They may also serve mezedes.

σουβλατζίδικο (soovlatz**ee**dheeko) Take-aways selling mainly pork kebabs (soovl**a**kee) and chips.

καφενείο (kafen**ee**o) Traditional coffee shop which is often a social centre for the men of a village.

εστιατόριο (esteeat**o**reeo) Restaurant.

ρεστοράν (restor**a**n) Restaurants in tourist resorts usually start serving food from midday or 1 p.m. until late at night. Greeks tend to have a large meal for lunch between 1 and 3 p.m. If going out for dinner, they tend to do so after 8 or 9 p.m.

ζαχαροπλαστείο (zakharoplast**ee**o) Patisserie selling sweet Greek pastries either to take away or to eat on the premises. They usually also serve coffee and soft drinks.

χώρος για πικνίκ (kh**o**ros ya picnic) Picnic area.

In a bar/café

If you ask for a coffee you are likely to be served a Greek (Turkish) coffee. If you like it sweet ask for **καφέ γλυκό** (kaf**e** gleek**o**), medium sweet is **καφέ μέτριο** (kaf**e** m**e**treeo) and without sugar is **καφέ σκέτο** (kaf**e** sk**e**to). If you want an instant coffee you will need to ask for **ένα νεσκαφέ** (**e**na neskaf**e**). A refreshing drink in the summer is an iced coffee. Ask for **καφέ φραπέ** (kaf**e** frap**e**) or for an espresso or a cappuccino **freddo** (cold).

FACE TO FACE

Τι θα πάρετε;
tee tha p**a**rete?
What will you have?

Ένα τσάι με γάλα παρακαλώ
ena ts**a**ee me gh**a**la parakal**o**
A tea with milk, please

a cappuccino	**ένα καπουτσίνο**	**e**na kapoots**ee**no
a beer	**μία μπύρα**	m**ee**a b**ee**ra
an ouzo	**ένα ούζο**	**e**na o**u**zo
...please	**...παρακαλώ**	...parakal**o**
a tea...	**ένα τσάι...**	**e**na ts**a**ee...
with lemon	**με λεμόνι**	me lem**o**nee
without sugar	**χωρίς ζάχαρη**	khor**ee**s z**a**kharee
for me	**για μένα**	ya m**e**na
for her	**γι' αυτήν**	yaft**ee**n
for him	**γι' αυτόν**	yaft**o**n
A bottle of mineral water	**Ένα μπουκάλι εμφιαλωμένο νερό**	**e**na book**a**lee emfeealom**e**no ner**o**
sparkling	**αεριούχο**	aeree**oo**kho
still	**απλό**	apl**o**

Tap water is generally safe except in small villages and on some islands. It is best to ask beforehand. Bottled water is widely available and fairly cheap in comparison to other European countries.

Other drinks to try

a lemon juice	**ένα χυμό λεμονιού** **e**na kheem**o** lemony**oo**
an orange juice	**ένα χυμό πορτοκαλιού** **e**na kheem**o** portokaly**oo**
a glass of retsina	**ένα ποτήρι ρετσίνα** **e**na pot**ee**ree rets**ee**na
a brandy	**ένα κονιάκ** **e**na kony**a**k
a soft drink	**ένα αναψυκτικό** **e**na anapseekteek**o**

In a restaurant

Restaurants and **tavernas** are welcoming, family-friendly places. In popular tourist destinations, they are open all day. In cities, restaurants are open from the early evening, but it is advisable to book a table. In **tavernas** the service can be slow but you won't be rushed out either. On some islands it is customary to serve guests fruit, sweets or a shot of liquor at the end of a meal. Even if service charge is included, a small tip is always appreciated. If there is no charge, you should leave at least 10% .

Θα ήθελα ένα τραπέζι για ... άτομα
tha **ee**thela **e**na trap**e**zee ya ... **a**toma
I'd like to book a table for ... people

Ναι, για πότε;
ne, ya p**o**te?
Yes, when for?

Για απόψε.../Για αύριο βράδυ...
ya ap**o**pse.../ya **a**vreeo vr**a**dee...
For tonight.../For tomorrow night...

The menu, please	**Τον κατάλογο, παρακαλώ** ton kat**a**logho, parakal**o**
What is the dish of the day?	**Ποιο είναι το πιάτο της ημέρας;** pyo **ee**ne to py**a**to tees eem**e**ras?
Is there a children's menu?	**Υπάρχει παιδικό μενού;** eep**a**rkhee pedheek**o** men**oo**?
I'll have this	**Θα πάρω αυτό** tha p**a**ro aft**o**
Excuse me!	**Με συγχωρείτε!** me seenkhor**ee**te!
Please bring...	**Παρακαλώ, φέρτε...** parakal**o** f**e**rte...
more bread	**κι άλλο ψωμί** kee **a**lo psom**ee**
more water	**κι άλλο νερό** kee **a**lo ner**o**

another bottle	**άλλο ένα μπουκάλι**	
	alo **e**na book**a**lee	
the bill	**το λογαριασμό**	
	to loghare**e**asm**o**	
a high chair	**μία παιδική καρέκλα**	
	m**ee**a pedheek**ee** kar**e**kla	
Is there a set menu?	**Έχετε προκαθορισμένο μενού (σετ μενού);**	
	ekhete prokathoreesm**e**no men**u** (set men**u**)	
We would like a table for ... people please	**Θα θέλαμε ένα τραπέζι για ... παρακαλώ**	
	tha th**e**lame **e**na trap**e**zee y**a** ... parakal**o**	
This isn't what I ordered	**Δεν είναι αυτό που παράγγειλα**	
	dhen **ee**ne aft**o** poo par**a**ngheela	
The ... is too...	**Το/Η ... είναι πολύ...**	
	to/ee ... **ee**ne pol**ee**...	

cold	**κρύο/κρύα**	kr**ee**o/kr**ee**a
greasy	**πολύ λιπαρό/ λιπαρή**	pol**ee** leepar**o**/ leepar**ee**
rare	**μισοψημένο**	meesopseem**e**no
salty	**αλμυρό/ αλμυρή**	almeer**o** / almeer**ee**
spicy	**με καρυκεύματα**	me kareek**e**vmata
warm	**ζεστό/ζεστή**	zest**o**/zest**ee**
well cooked	**καλοψημένο**	kalopseem**e**no

Reading the menu

A Greek meal usually consists of one substantial main course, often with chips and salad, followed by a simple dessert such as fresh fruit. Bread is absolutely compulsory and Greeks often order a few side dishes to share.

χειροποίητο kheerop**ee-e**eto	homemade
τοπική λιχουδιά topeek**ee** leekhoodhee**a**	local delicacy

Starters **Ορεκτικά** (orekteek**a**)

τζατζίκι (tzatz**ee**kee) yoghurt, cucumber, and garlic dip

ταραμοσαλάτα (taramosal**a**ta) dip made from fish roe

ελιές (ely**e**s) olives usually marinated in olive oil and garlic

γιαούρτι (ya**oo**rtee) yogurt

καλαμάρια (kalam**a**rya) sliced squid in batter

κεφτέδες (keft**e**dhes) meat balls

αγγουροντομάτα (angoorondom**a**ta) tomato and cucumber salad

φέτα (f**e**ta) feta cheese

χταπόδι (khtap**o**dhee) octopus

λουκάνικο (look**a**neeko) sausage

Greek dishes you might like to try

ντολμαδάκια (dolmadh**a**kya) stuffed vineleaves

πιπεριές γεμιστές (peepery**e**s yemeest**e**s)
stuffed peppers

παστίτσιο (past**ee**tsyo) layers of pasta and minced
meat, with a white sauce topping

μουσακάς (moossak**a**s) layers of aubergine and
minced meat

γιουβέτσι (yoov**e**tsee) roast lamb with pasta

στιφάδο (steef**a**dho) beef and onions

Meat and poultry
Κρέας και πουλερικά (kr**e**as ke poolereek**a**)

μπριζόλα μοσχαρίσια (breez**o**la
moskhar**ee**sya) beefsteak

μπριζόλα χοιρινή (breez**o**la kheereen**ee**)
pork chop

σουβλάκι χοιρινό (soovl**a**kee kheereen**o**)
pork kebab

σουβλάκι αρνίσιο (soovl**a**kee arn**ee**syo)
lamb kebab

παϊδάκια αρνίσια (paeedh**a**kya arn**ee**sya)
lamb chops

μοσχάρι ψητό (moskharee pseeto) roast beef

κοτόπουλο ψητό (kotopoolo pseeto) roast chicken

Fish **Ψάρια** (psareea)

γαρίδες (ghareedhes) prawns

μπαρμπούνι (barboonee) red mullet

λιθρίνι (leethreenee) grey mullet

αστακός (astakos) lobster

ξιφίας (kseefeeas) swordfish

γλώσσα (ghlosa) sole

σουπιές (soopyes) cuttlefish

λαβράκι (lavrakee) sea bass

τσιπούρα (tseepoora) sea bream

Eggs **Αβγά** (avgha)

αβγά τηγανητά (avgha teeghaneeta) fried eggs

αβγά βραστά (avgha vrasta) boiled eggs

ομελέτα (omeleta) omelette

αβγά ζαμπόν (avgha zambon) ham and eggs

Vegetables **Λαχανικά** (lakhaneeka)

μπάμιες (bamyes) okra, 'lady's fingers'

σπανάκι (spanakee) spinach

κολοκυθάκια (kolokeethakya) courgettes

μελιτζάνες (meleetzanes) aubergines

καρότα (kar**o**ta) carrots

αγγούρι (ang**oo**ree) cucumber

ντομάτα (dom**a**ta) tomato

μαρούλι (mar**oo**lee) lettuce

πατάτες (pat**a**tes) potatoes

πατάτες τηγανητές (pat**a**tes teeghaneet**e**s) chips

πατάτες πουρέ (pat**a**tes poor**e**) mashed potatoes

πατάτες φούρνου (pat**a**tes f**oo**rnoo)
roast potatoes

Fruit **Φρούτα** (fr**oo**ta)

σταφύλια (staf**ee**lya) grapes

καρπούζι (karp**oo**zee) watermelon

πεπόνι (pep**o**nee) melon

σύκα (s**ee**ka) figs

αχλάδια (akhl**a**dhya) pears

μήλα (m**ee**la) apples

κεράσια (ker**a**sya) cherries

ροδάκινα (rodh**a**keena) peaches

βερίκοκα (ver**ee**koka) apricots

φράουλες (fr**a**ooles) strawberries

μπανάνες (ban**a**nes) bananas

Desserts **Γλυκά** (ghleek**a**)

A Greek meal is rarely followed by a sweet dessert. Although dessert may be served at some restaurants, it is more common to have fresh fruit. The place to go for Greek sweets is the patisserie, **ζαχαροπλαστείο** (zakharoplast**ee**o).

πάστες (p**a**stes) slices of gateaux

μπακλαβάς (baklav**a**s) filo pastry filled with chopped almonds, in syrup

καταΐφι (kata**ee**fee) shredded pastry with a filling of chopped almonds, in syrup

παγωτό (paghot**o**) ice cream

γαλακτομπούρεκο (ghalaktob**oo**reko) filo pastry with a cream filling, in syrup

κομπόστα (kob**o**sta) stewed or tinned fruit

Dietary requirements

· ·

Are there any vegetarian restaurants here?	**Υπάρχουν καθόλου εστιατόρια για χορτοφάγους εδώ;** eep**a**rkhoon kath**o**loo esteeat**o**reea ya khortof**a**ghoos edh**o**?

Do you have any vegetarian dishes?	Έχετε καθόλου φαγητά για χορτοφάγους; ekhete katholoo fa-yeeta ya khortofaghoos?
What fish dishes do you have?	Τι φαγητά με ψάρια έχετε; tee fa-yeeta me psarya ekhete?
I don't like meat	Δεν μου αρέσει το κρέας dhen moo aresee to kreas
What do you recommend?	Τι προτείνετε; tee proteenete?
I have a ... allergy	Έχω αλλεργία στη/στους... ekho alleryeea stee/stoos...
I don't eat...	Δεν τρώω... dhen troo...

coeliac	η κοιλιοκάκη	keeleeokakee
dairy	τα γαλακτοκομικά προιόντα	ta ghalaktokomeeka proeeonta
gluten	η γλουτένη	ghlootenee
halal	μέθοδος halal σύμφωνη με την ισλαμική παράδοση	methodhos halal seemfonee me teen eeslameekee paradhosee
nuts	οι ξηροί καρποί	ee kseeree karpee
organic	βιολογικό	veeologheeko
vegan	ακραιφνής χορτοφάγος	akrefnees khortofaghos
wheat	το σιτάρι	to seetaree

114

Wines and spirits

. . . .

The wine list, please	**Τον κατάλογο των κρασιών, παρακαλώ** ton kat**a**logho ton krasy**o**n, parakal**o**
Can you recommend a good wine?	**Μπορείτε να μας προτείνετε ένα καλό κρασί;** bor**ee**te na mas prot**ee**nete **e**na kal**o** kras**ee**?
A bottle...	**Ένα μπουκάλι...** **e**na book**a**lee...
A carafe...	**Μία καράφα...** m**ee**a kar**a**fa...
of (house) wine	**κρασί** kras**ee**
of red wine	**κόκκινο κρασί** k**o**keeno kras**ee**
of white wine	**λευκό κρασί** lefk**o** kras**ee**
of rosé wine	**κρασί ροζέ** kras**ee** roz**e**
of sweet wine	**γλυκό κρασί** ghleek**o** kras**ee**
of a local wine	**τοπικό κρασί** topeek**o** kras**ee**

Eating out

Wines

Χατζημιχάλη (khadzeemeekhalee) a range of wines from Northern Greece

Αχαία Κλάους (akhaya klaoos) a range of wines from the Peloponnese

Αβέρωφ (averof) red wines from Epirus

Τσάνταλη (tsantalee) a selection of wines from Thrace and Macedonia

Αγιορείτικο (ayoreeteeko) wine made by monks on Mt Athos

Μαυροδάφνη (mavrodhafnee) a sweet red dessert wine

Μόντε Χρήστος (monte khreestos) a sweet red wine from Cyprus

Αφροδίτη (afrodheetee) a medium white wine from Cyprus

Σάμος (samos) traditional dessert wine from the Aegean island of Samos

Νεμέας (nemeas) dry red wine from Nemea, Peloponnese

Spirits

κονιάκ (kony**a**k) brandy, ranked by a star system: the more stars, the better quality the brandy

ούζο (**oo**zo) an aniseed-flavoured colourless drink, drunk on its own or with water. When water is added it turns white

ρακή (rak**ee**) a clear strong spirit

Other drinks to try

ρετσίνα (rets**ee**na) a resinated white wine which can accompany a meal but can equally well be enjoyed on its own, especially well chilled or with soda, lemonade or Coke

κουμανταρία (koomantar**ee**a) very sweet dessert wine from Cyprus

φιλφάρ (feelf**a**r) an orange-flavoured liqueur from Cyprus

Menu reader

α A

αεριούχο aeree**oo**kho fizzy, sparkling

αθερίνα ather**ee**na whitebait, usually fried

αρνί γιουβέτσι arn**ee** yoov**e**tsee roast lamb with small pasta

αρνί λεμονάτο arn**ee** lemon**a**to lamb braised in sauce with herbs and lemon juice

αρνί ψητό arn**ee** pseet**o** roast lamb

αστακός astak**o**s lobster (often served with lemon juice and olive oil)

άσπρο κρασί **a**spro kras**ee** white wine

αυγολέμονο avghol**e**mono egg and lemon soup

αφέλια af**e**leea pork in red wine with seasonings

β B

βλήτα vl**ee**ta wild greens (like spinach, eaten with olive oil and lemon)

βουτήματα voot**ee**mata biscuits to dip in coffee

βραδινό vradeen**o** evening meal

βραστό vrast**o** boiled

γ Γ

γαλακτομπούρεκο ghalaktob**oo**reko custard tart

γαρίδες ghar**ee**dhes shrimps; prawns

γαύρος gavros sardine-type fish (if salted: anchovy)

γίδα βραστή y**ee**da vrast**ee** goat soup

γεμιστά yemeest**a** stuffed vegetables

γιαούρτι ya**oo**rtee yoghurt

γιαούρτι με μέλι ya**oo**rtee me m**e**lee yoghurt with honey

γιαχνί yakhn**ee** cooked in tomato sauce and olive oil

γίγαντες y**ee**ghantes large broad beans baked in tomato sauce with herbs

γιουβαρλάκια yoovarl**a**kya meatballs in lemon sauce

γλυκά κουταλιού ghleek**a** kootaly**oo** crystallized fruits in syrup

γλώσσα ghl**o**sa sole

γόπες gh**o**pes bogue, a type of fish

γραβιέρα ghravy**e**ra cheese resembling gruyère

γύρος y**ee**ros doner kebab

δ Δ

δείπνο dh**ee**pno dinner

δίπλες dh**ee**ples pastry with honey and walnuts

ε E

ελάχιστα ψημένο elakheesta pseemeno rare (meat)

ελαιόλαδο eleoladho olive oil

ελιές τσακιστές elyes tsakeestes cracked green olives with coriander seeds and garlic (Cyprus)

εξοχικό eksokheeko stuffed pork or beef with vegetables and cheese

ζ Z

ζεστή σοκολάτα zestee sokolata hot chocolate

ζεστό zesto hot, warm

θ Θ

Θαλασσινά thalaseena seafood

ι I

ιμάμ μπαϊλντί eemam baeeldee stuffed aubergines

κ K

κάβα kava wine shop

καγιανάς με παστό κρέας kayanas me pasto kreas salted pork with cheese, tomatoes and eggs

κακαβιά kakavya fish soup

κακάο kakow hot chocolate

καλαμάκι kalam**a**kee straw (for drinking); small skewer

καλαμάρια kalam**a**rya squid

καλοψημένο kalopseem**e**no well done (meat)

κάπαρι k**a**paree pickled capers

καπνιστό kapneest**o** smoked

καπουτσίνο kapoots**ee**no cappucino

καράφα kar**a**fa carafe

καρυδόπιτα kareedh**o**peeta walnut cake

κασέρι kas**e**ree type of cheese

καταΐφι kata**ee**fee small shredded pastry drenched in syrup

κατάλογος kat**a**loghos menu

κατάλογος κρασιών kat**a**loghos krasy**o**n wine list

καταψυγμένο katapseeghm**e**no frozen

κατσίκι kats**ee**kee roast kid

καφενείο kafen**ee**o café

καφές kaf**e**s coffee (Greek-style)

καφέδες kaf**e**dhes coffees (plural)

καφές γλυκός kaf**e**s ghleek**o**s very sweet coffee

καφές μέτριος kaf**e**s m**e**treeos medium-sweet coffee

καφές σκέτος kaf**e**s sk**e**tos coffee without sugar

κεράσια ker**a**sya cherries

κεφαλοτύρι kefalot**ee**ree type of cheese, often served fried in olive oil

κεφτέδες keft**e**dhes meat balls

κιμάς keem**a**s mince

κλέφτικο kl**e**fteeko casserole with lamb, potatoes and vegetables

κοκορέτσι kokor**e**tsee traditional spit-roasted dish of spiced liver and other offal

κολοκυθάκια kolokeeth**a**kya courgettes

κολοκυθόπιτα kolokeeth**o**peeta courgette pie

κονιάκ kony**a**k brandy, cognac

κοντοσούβλι kontos**oo**vlee spicy pieces of lamb, pork or beef, spit-roasted

κουλούρια kool**oo**rya bread rings

κουπέπια koop**e**pya stuffed vine leaves (Cyprus)

κούπες k**oo**pes meat pasties

κουραμπιέδες koorambγ**e**dhes small almond cakes eaten at Christmas

κρητική σαλάτα kreeteek**ee** sal**a**ta watercress salad

κρύο kr**ee**o cold

κυνήγι keen**ee**ghee game

κύριο πιάτο k**ee**reeo py**a**to main course

λ Λ

λαδότυρο ladh**o**teero soft cheese with olive oil

λάχανα l**a**khana green vegetables

λάχανο l**a**khano cabbage, greens

λεμονάδα lemon**a**dha lemon drink

λευκό lefk**o** white (used for wine as well as **άσπρο**)

λίγο l**ee**gho a little, a bit

λουκάνικα look**a**neeka type of highly seasoned sausage

λουκουμάδες lookoom**a**dhes small fried dough balls in syrup

λουκούμι look**oo**mee Turkish delight

λούντζα l**oo**ndza loin of pork, marinated and smoked

μ M

μαγειρίτσα mayeer**ee**tsa soup made of lamb offal, special Easter dish

μακαρόνια με κιμά makar**o**nya me keem**a** spaghetti bolognese

μαρίδες mar**ee**dhes small fish like sprats, served fried

μαύρο κρασί m**a**vro kras**ee** red wine (although you'll hear k**o**keeno kras**ee** more often)

μανιτάρια maneet**a**rya mushrooms

μαυρομάτικα mavrom**a**teeka black-eyed beans

μεγάλο megh**a**lo large, big

μεζές mez**e**s (plural **μεζέδες** mez**e**dhes) small snacks served free of charge with ouzo or retsina; assortment of mini-portions of various dishes, available on the menu (or on request) at some restaurants

μεζεδοπωλείο mezedhopol**ee**o taverna/shop selling **μεζέδες** (mez**e**dhes)

μελιτζάνα meleetza**na** aubergine

μελιτζάνες ιμάμ meleetza**nes** eem**am** aubergines stuffed with tomato and onion

μελιτζανοσαλάτα meleetzanos**a**lata aubergine mousse (dip)

μεσημεριανό meseemeryan**o** lunch

μεταλλικό νερό metaleek**o** ner**o** mineral water

Μεταξά metaks**a** Metaxa (Greek brandy-type spirit)

μέτρια ψημένο m**e**treea pseem**e**no medium-grilled (meat)

μη αεριούχο mee aereе**oo**kho still, not fizzy

μηλόπιτα meel**o**peeta apple pie

μοσχάρι moskh**a**ree beef

μοσχάρι κοκκινιστό moskh**a**ree kokeeneest**o** beef in wine sauce with tomatoes and onions

μουσακάς moosak**a**s moussaka, layers of aubergine minced meat and potato, with white sauce

μπακαλιάρος παστός bakaly**a**ros past**o**s salt cod

μπακλαβάς baklav**a**s filo-pastry with nuts soaked in syrup

μπάμιες b**a**myes okra, ladies' fingers (vegetable)

μπιφτέκι beeft**e**kee beef rissole/burger

μπουγάτσα boogh**a**tsa cheese or custard pastry sprinkled with sugar and cinnamon

μπουρέκι boor**e**kee cheese, potato and courgette pie

μπουρέκια boor**e**kya puff pastry filled with meat and cheese (Cyprus)

μπριάμ(ι) bree**a**m(ee) ratatouille

μπριζόλα breez**o**la steak/chop

μπριζόλα αρνίσια breez**o**la arn**ee**sya lamb chop

μπριζόλα μοσχαρίσια breez**o**la moskhar**ee**sya beef steak/chop

μπριζόλα χοιρινή breez**o**la kheereen**ee** pork chop

μπύρα b**ee**ra beer

ν N

νες, νεσκαφέ nes, nescaf**e** instant coffee (of any brand)

νες με γάλα nes me gh**a**la coffee (instant) with milk

νες φραπέ nes frapp**e** iced coffee

ντολμάδες dolm**a**dhes vine leaves, rolled up and stuffed with rice and sometimes mince

ντομάτες γεμιστές dom**a**tes yemeest**es** tomatoes stuffed with rice and herbs, and sometimes with mince

ξ Ξ

ξιφίας kseef**ee**as swordfish

ο Ο

ομελέτα omel**e**tta omelette

ορεκτικά orekteek**a** first courses/starters (menu heading)

ουζερί oozer**ee** small bar selling ouzo and other drinks, maybe with **μεζέδες** (mez**e**dhes)

ούζο oo**z**o ouzo (traditional aniseed-flavoured spirit)

οχταπόδι okhtap**o**dhee octopus (see also **χταπόδι**)

οχταπόδι κρασάτο okhtap**o**dhee krasato octopus in red wine sauce

π Π

παγάκια pagh**a**kya ice-cubes

παϊδάκια paeedh**a**kya grilled lamb chops

παντζάρια pandz**a**rya beetroot with seasonings

παξιμάδια pakseem**a**dhya crispy bread (baked twice)

παπουτσάκια papoots**a**kya stuffed aubergines

πάστα p**a**sta cake, pastry

παστό past**o** salted

παστιτσάδα pasteets**a**da beef with tomatoes, onions, red wine, herbs, spices and pasta

παστίτσιο past**ee**tseeo baked pasta dish with a middle layer of meat and white sauce

πατσάς pats**a**s tripe soup

πατάτες τηγανιτές pat**a**tes teeghaneet**e**s chips, fries

πιάτο της ημέρας p**ya**to tees eem**e**ras dish of the day

πιπεριές γεμιστές peepery**e**s yemeest**e**s stuffed peppers with rice, herbs and sometimes mince

πίτα or **πίττα** p**ee**ta pitta (flat unleavened bread); pie with different fillings, such as meat, cheese, vegetables

πλακί plak**ee** fish in tomato sauce

πουργούρι poorgh**oo**ree cracked wheat (Cyprus)

πουργούρι πιλάφι poorgh**oo**ree peel**a**fee salad made of cracked wheat (Cyprus)

πρωινό proeen**o** breakfast

ρ P

ραβιόλι ravy**o**lee pastry stuffed with cheese (Cyprus)

ρακή, ρακί rak**ee** raki, strong spirit a bit like schnapps

ρέγγα καπνιστή r**e**nga kapneest**ee** smoked herring, kipper

ρετσίνα rets**ee**na retsina, traditional resinated white wine

ρίγανη r**ee**ghanee oregano

ροζέ κρασί roz**e** kras**ee** rosé wine

ρυζόγαλο reez**o**ghalo rice pudding

σ ς Σ

σαγανάκι saghan**a**kee cheese coated in flour and fried in olive oil

127

σαλιγκάρια saleeng**a**rya snails

σεφταλιά seftaly**a** minced pork sausage (Cyprus)

σικαλένιο ψωμί seekal**e**nyo psom**ee** rye bread

σικώτι seek**o**tee liver

σκορδαλιά skordhaly**a** garlic and potato mash

σκορδαλιά με ψάρι τηγανιτό skordhaly**a** me ps**a**ree teeghaneet**o** fried fish served with garlic and potato mash

σουβλάκι soovl**a**kee meat (often pork) kebab skewers

σουβλατζίδικο soovlatz**ee**dheeko shop selling souvlakia, doner kebabs, etc.

σουπιά soopy**a** cuttlefish

σουτζουκάκια sootzook**a**kya highly seasoned meat balls

σπανάκι span**a**kee spinach

σπανακόπιτα spanak**o**peeta spinach pie

σπαράγγια σαλάτα spar**a**ngya sal**a**ta asparagus salad

στη σούβλα stee s**oo**vla spit-roasted

στιφάδο steef**a**dho braised beef in spicy onion and tomato sauce

στο φούρνο sto f**oo**rno baked in the oven

στρείδια str**ee**dhya oysters

σχάρας skh**a**ras grilled

τ Τ

ταραμοσαλάτα taramosal**a**ta mousse of cod roe

τζατζίκι tzatz**ee**kee yoghurt, garlic and cucumber dip

τηγανιτό teeghaneet**o** fried

τραχανάς trahan**a**s soup made of cracked wheat and yoghurt (Cyprus)

τσιπούρα tseep**oo**ra a type of sea bream

τσουρέκι tsoor**e**kee festive bread

τυροκαυτερή teerokafter**ee** spicy dip made of cheese and peppers

τυρόπιτα teer**o**peeta cheese pie

τυροσαλάτα teerosal**a**ta starter made of cream cheese and herbs

φ Φ

φάβα f**a**va yellow split peas or lentils, served in a purée with olive oil and capers

φασολάδα fasol**a**dha soup made with white beans and vegetables, eaten with lemon

φασολάκια fasol**a**kya green beans

φασόλια fas**o**lya haricot beans

φέτα f**e**ta feta cheese, tangy white cheese used in salads and other dishes; a slice

φλαούνες fla**oo**nes Easter cheese (Cyprus)

φραπέ frap**e** iced coffee

φρέσκο fr**e**sko fresh

χ X

χαλβάς khalv**a**s sesame seed sweet

χαλούμι khal**oo**mee ewe's or goat's-milk cheese, often grilled

χόρτα kh**o**rta wild greens (similar to spinach) eaten cold with oil and lemon

χορτοφάγος khortof**a**ghos vegetarian

χούμους kh**oo**moos dip made with puréed chickpeas, hummus (Cyprus)

χταπόδι khtap**o**dhee octopus, grilled or as a side-salad

χωριάτικη σαλάτα khory**a**teekee sal**a**ta Greek-style salad, with tomatoes, feta cheese, cucumber, onions, olives and oregano

ψ Ψ

ψάρια καπνιστά ps**a**rya kapneest**a** smoked fish

ψάρια πλακί ps**a**rya plak**ee** baked whole fish with vegetables and tomatoes

ψαρόσουπα psar**o**soopa seafood soup

ψαροταβέρνα psarotav**e**rna fish taverna

ψησταριά pseestary**a** grill house

ψητό pseet**o** roast/grilled

ψωμί ολικής αλέσεως psom**ee** oleek**ee**s al**e**seos wholemeal bread

Reference

Measurements and quantities

• •

1 lb = approx. 0.5 kilo
1 pint = approx. 0.5 litre

Liquids

1/2 litre of...	**μισό λίτρο...**
	mees**o** l**ee**tro...
a litre of...	**ένα λίτρο...**
	ena l**ee**tro...
a bottle of...	**ένα μπουκάλι...**
	ena book**a**lee...
a glass of...	**ένα ποτήρι...**
	ena pot**ee**ree...

Weights

100 grams	**εκατό γραμμάρια**
	ekat**o** ghram**a**reea
1/2 kilo of...	**μισό κιλό...**
(500 g)	mees**o** keel**o**...
a kilo of...	**ένα κιλό...**
(1000 g)	**e**na keel**o**...

Food

a slice of...	**μια φέτα...** mya feta...
a portion of...	**μια μερίδα...** mya mereedha...
a box of...	**ένα κουτί...** ena kootee...
a packet of...	**ένα πακέτο...** ena paketo...
a tin of...	**μια κονσέρβα...** mya konserva...
a jar of...	**ένα βάζο...** ena vazo...

Miscellaneous

10 euros	**δέκα ευρώ** dheka evro
20 cents	**είκοσι λεπτά** eekosee lepta
a third	**ένα τρίτο** ena treeto
a quarter	**ένα τέταρτο** ena tetarto
ten per cent	**δέκα τοις εκατό** dheka tees ekato
more...	**περισσότερο...** pereesotero...

less...	**λιγότερο...**
	leeghotero...
enough	**αρκετό**
	arketo
double	**διπλό**
	dheeplo
twice	**διπλάσιο**
	dheeplaseeo
three times	**τριπλάσιο**
	treeplaseeo

Numbers

. . . .

0	**μηδέν** meedhen
1	**ένα** ena
2	**δύο** dheeo
3	**τρία** treea
4	**τέσσερα** tesera
5	**πέντε** pende
6	**έξι** eksee
7	**εφτά** efta
8	**οχτώ** okhto
9	**εννιά** enya
10	**δέκα** dheka
11	**έντεκα** endeka

12	**δώδεκα** dhodheka
13	**δεκατρία** dhekatreea
14	**δεκατέσσερα** dhekatesera
15	**δεκαπέντε** dhekapende
16	**δεκαέξι** dhekaeksee
17	**δεκαεφτά** dhekaefta
18	**δεκαοχτώ** dhekaokhto
19	**δεκαεννιά** dhekaenya
20	**είκοσι** eekosee
21	**είκοσι ένα** eekosee ena
22	**είκοσι δύο** eekosee dheeo
30	**τριάντα** treeanda
40	**σαράντα** saranda
50	**πενήντα** peneenda
60	**εξήντα** ekseenda
70	**εβδομήντα** evdhomeenda
80	**ογδόντα** oghdhonda
90	**ενενήντα** eneneenda
100	**εκατό** ekato
110	**εκατόν δέκα** ekaton dheka
500	**πεντακόσια** pendakosya
1,000	**χίλια** kheelya
2,000	**δύο χιλιάδες** dheeo kheelyadhes
1 million	**ένα εκατομμύριο** ena ekatomeereeo

1st	**πρώτος**	6th	**έκτος**
	protos		ektos
2nd	**δεύτερος**	7th	**έβδομος**
	dhefteros		evdhomos
3rd	**τρίτος**	8th	**όγδοος**
	treetos		oghdho-os
4th	**τέταρτος**	9th	**ένατος**
	tetartos		enatos
5th	**πέμπτος**	10th	**δέκατος**
	pemptos		dhekatos

Days and months

. . . .

Days

Monday	**Δευτέρα**	dheftera
Tuesday	**Τρίτη**	treetee
Wednesday	**Τετάρτη**	tetartee
Thursday	**Πέμπτη**	pemptee
Friday	**Παρασκευή**	paraskevee
Saturday	**Σάββατο**	savato
Sunday	**Κυριακή**	keeryakee

Months

January	**Ιανουάριος**	eeanoo**a**reeos
February	**Φεβρουάριος**	fevroo**a**reeos
March	**Μάρτιος**	m**a**rteeos
April	**Απρίλιος**	apr**ee**leeos
May	**Μάιος**	m**a**eeos
June	**Ιούνιος**	ee**oo**neeos
July	**Ιούλιος**	ee**oo**leeos
August	**Αύγουστος**	**av**ghoostos
September	**Σεπτέμβριος**	sept**e**mvreeos
October	**Οκτώβριος**	okt**o**vreeos
November	**Νοέμβριος**	no**e**mvreeos
December	**Δεκέμβριος**	dhek**e**mvreeos

Seasons

spring	**Άνοιξη**	**a**neeksee
summer	**Καλοκαίρι**	kalok**e**ree
autumn	**Φθινόπωρο**	ftheen**o**poro
winter	**Χειμώνας**	kheem**o**nas

What's the date?	**Τι ημερομηνία έχουμε;**
	tee eemeromeen**ee**a **e**khoome?
It's the 5th of August 2016	**Είναι η 5η Αυγούστου 2016**
	eene ee p**e**mptee avgh**oo**stoo dh**ee**o kheelee**a**des dh**e**ka **e**ksee

on Saturday	**το Σάββατο**
	to s**a**vato
on Saturdays	**τα Σάββατα**
	ta s**a**vata
this Saturday	**αυτό το Σάββατο**
	aft**o** to s**a**vato
next Saturday	**το επόμενο Σάββατο**
	to ep**o**meno s**a**vato
last Saturday	**το περασμένο Σάββατο**
	to perasm**e**no s**a**vato
in June	**τον Ιούνιο**
	ton ee**oo**neeo
at the beginning of June	**στις αρχές Ιουνίου**
	stees arkh**e**s eeoon**ee**oo
at the end of June	**στα τέλη Ιουνίου**
	sta t**e**lee eeoon**ee**oo
before summer	**πριν από το καλοκαίρι**
	preen ap**o** to kalok**e**ree
during the summer	**μέσα στο καλοκαίρι**
	m**e**sa sto kalok**e**ree
after summer	**μετά το καλοκαίρι**
	met**a** to kalok**e**ree

Time

• •

When telling the time in Greek, remember that the hour comes first, then 'past' **και** (ke) or 'to' **παρά** (par**a**) and finally the minutes, e.g. 8.10 **οκτώ και δέκα** (okt**o** ke dh**e**ka) – ten past eight, 11.40 **δώδεκα παρά είκοσι** (dh**o**dheka par**a** ee**kose**e) – twenty to twelve.

What time is it, please?	**Τι ώρα είναι, παρακαλώ;** tee **o**ra **e**ene, parakal**o**?	
a.m.	**πμ** preen to meseem**e**ree	
p.m.	**μμ** met**a** to meseem**e**ree	
It's...	**Είναι...** **e**ene...	
2 o'clock	**δύο η ώρα** dh**ee**o ee **o**ra	
3 o'clock	**τρεις η ώρα** trees ee **o**ra	
It's 1 o'clock	**Είναι μία η ώρα** **e**ene m**ee**a ee **o**ra	
It's 12.00	**Είναι δώδεκα** **e**ene dh**o**dheka	
midday	**το μεσημέρι** to meseem**e**ree	

midnight	**τα μεσάνυχτα** ta mesaneekhta
9	**εννέα** enea
9.10	**εννέα και δέκα** enea ke dheka
quarter past 9	**εννέα και τέταρτο** enea ke tetarto
9.20	**εννέα και είκοσι** enea ke eekosee
9.30	**εννέα και μισή** enea ke meesee
9.35	**εννέα και τριάντα πέντε** enea ke treeanta pente
quarter to 10	**δέκα παρά τέταρτο** dheka para tetarto
10 to 10	**δέκα παρά δέκα** dheka para dheka

Time phrases

When does it open/close?	**Πότε ανοίγει/κλείνει;** poteaneeyee/kleenee?
When does it begin/finish?	**Πότε αρχίζει/τελειώνει;** potearkheezee/teleeonee?
at 3 o'clock	**στις τρεις η ώρα** steestrees ee ora
before 3 o'clock	**πριν από τις τρεις** preenapo tees trees
after 3 o'clock	**μετά τις τρεις** metatees trees
today	**σήμερα** seemera
tonight	**απόψε** apopse
tomorrow	**αύριο** avreeo
yesterday	**χθες** khthes

Public holidays

. . . .

January 1	**Πρωτοχρονιά** New Year's Day
January 6	**Θεοφάνεια** Epiphany
Late February/ early March	**Καθαρά Δευτέρα (Αρχή Σαρακοστής)** Ash Monday (40 days before Easter)
March 25	**Ο Ευαγγελισμός/Εθνική γιορτή της Ανεξαρτησίας** Annunciation and Greek Independence Day
April/May	**Πάσχα** Easter(Good Friday to Easter Monday)
May 1	**Εργατική Ημέρα Πρωτομαγιάς** Labour Day
May/June	**Πεντηκοστή** Whit Monday
August 15	**Ανάληψη (της Παναγίας)** Assumption (of the Virgin Mary)
October 28	**Ημέρα του "Όχι"** The "Ochi" Day: 2nd World War Memorial Day
December 25	**Χριστούγεννα** Christmas Day
December 26	**Δεύτερη Ημέρα των Χριστουγέννων** Boxing Day/St Stephen's Day

Reference

Phonetic map

· ·

When travelling in Greece, you will need to bear in mind that place names as we know them are not necessarily the same in Greek. Imagine if you wanted to buy tickets at a train station but couldn't see your destination on the departures list! This handy map eliminates such problems by indicating the locations and local pronunciations of major towns, cities and islands.

Thessalo

Koz

Larissa

Θεσσαλονίκη
Thessaloníki
thesalon**ee**kee

Κέρκυρα
Kérkyra
k**e**rkeera

Corfu

Κοζάνη
Kozáni
koz**a**nee

Pat

Λάρισα
Lárissa
l**a**reesa

Πάτρα
Pátra
p**a**tra

Αλεξανδρούπολη
Alexandroúpoli
aleksandr**oo**polee

● Alexandroupoli

Skiathos
Σκιάθος
Skíathos
sk**ee**athos

Λέσβος
Lésvos
lesvos

Lesbos

bes

Θήβα
Thíva
th**ee**va

Αθήνα
Athína
ath**ee**na

Athens

Piraeus

Mykonos
Μύκονος
Míkonos
m**ee**konos

Πειραιάς
Pireás
peer**eas**

Rhodes
Ρόδος
Ródos
rodos

Ηράκλειο
Iráklio
eer**a**kleeo

Heraklion

Κρήτη
Kríti
kr**ee**tee

Crete

Grammar

The following basic rules of Greek grammar will help you make full use of the information in this book.

Greek grammar is rather complicated by the fact that pronouns, nouns and adjectives change their endings according to their function in the sentence, their form (whether they are singular or plural) and their gender (whether they are masculine, feminine or neuter) – rather like German. A brief outline of the grammar is given here, but for a fuller explanation you should consult a Greek grammar book.

Nouns

A noun is a word used to refer to a person or thing, e.g. 'car', 'horse', 'Mary'. Greek nouns can be masculine, feminine or neuter, and the words for 'the' and 'a' (the articles) change according to the gender of the noun.

o (o)	= the with masculine nouns
η (ee)	= the with feminine nouns
το (to)	= the with neuter nouns

ένας (**e**nas)	= a with masculine nouns
μία (m**ee**a)	= a with feminine nouns
ένα (**e**na)	= a with neuter nouns

The article is the most reliable indication of the gender of a noun, i.e. whether it is masculine, feminine or neuter.

In the dictionary sections you will come across examples like this: **o/η γιατρός** (yatr**o**s) doctor.

This means that the same ending is used for men as well as women doctors i.e. **o γιατρός** is a male doctor, **η γιατρός** is a female doctor.

You will also encounter entries like **o Άγγλος/η Αγγλίδα** indicating that an Englishman is referred to as **o Άγγλος** (**a**nglos) while an Englishwoman is **η Αγγλίδα** (angl**ee**dha).

Masculine endings of nouns

The most common endings of masculine nouns are **-ος** (os), **-ας** (as), **-ης** (ees), e.g.

o καιρός (ker**o**s)	weather
o πατέρας (pat**e**ras)	father
o κυβερνήτης (keevern**ee**tees)	captain (of aeroplane)

Feminine endings of nouns

The most common endings of feminine nouns are
-α (a), **-η** (ee), e.g.

η μητέρα (meet**e**ra)   mother

η Κρήτη (kr**ee**tee)   Crete

Neuter endings of nouns

The most common neuter endings are: **-ο** (o),
-ι (ee), e.g.

το κτίριο (kt**ee**reeo)   building

το πορτοκάλι (portok**a**lee)   orange (fruit)

Plurals

• •

The article 'the' changes in the plural. For
masculine (**ο**) and feminine (**η**) nouns it becomes **οι**
(ee). For neuter nouns (**το**) it becomes **τα** (ta).

You may have noticed that nouns have different
endings in the plural. Masculine nouns change
their endings to **-οι** (ee), e.g.

ο βράχος (vr**a**khos)   **οι βράχοι** (vr**a**khee)

Feminine nouns change their endings to **-ες** (es), e.g.

η κυρία (ker**ee**a)   **οι κυρίες** (ker**ee**-es)

Neuter nouns change their endings to **-α** (a), e.g.

το κτίριο (kt**ee**reeo)   **τα κτίρια** (kt**ee**reea)

There are many exceptions to the above rules, such as:

ο άντρας (**a**ndhras)   **οι άντρες** (**a**ndhres)

Adjectives

. . . .

An adjective is a word that describes or gives extra information about a person or thing, e.g. 'small', 'pretty' or 'practical'. Greek adjectives have endings that change according to the gender and form of the noun they describe, e.g.:

ο καλός πατέρας
(kal**o**s pat**e**ras)   the good father

η καλή κυρία
(kal**ee** ker**ee**a)   the good lady

οι καλοί πατέρες
(kal**ee** pat**e**res)   the good fathers

οι καλές κυρίες
(kal**e**s ker**ee**-es)   the good ladies

In the Greek-English dictionary section of this book, all adjectives are given with their endings clearly shown, e.g.:

κρύος/α/ο (kr**ee**-os/a/o)cold

By far the most common adjective endings are **-ος** (os) for masculine, **-α** (a) for feminine and **-ο** (o) for neuter nouns.

Possessive adjectives

In Greek, adjectives go before the noun they describe, but the possessive adjectives (my, your, his, etc.) follow the noun. They don't change according to the gender and number of the noun. The article is still added in front of the noun.

my	**μου**	moo
your	**σου**	soo
his	**του**	too
her	**της**	tees
its	**του**	too
our	**μας**	mas
your (plural) (This is also the polite form)	**σας**	sas
their	**τους**	toos

| my key | **το κλειδί μου** (to kleeth**ee** moo) |
| your room | **το δωμάτιό σας** (to dhom**a**tee**o** sas) |

Verbs

· ·

A verb is a word used to describe an action (e.g. to sing), a state (e.g. to become) or an occurrence (e.g. to happen). Unlike verbs in English, Greek verbs have a different ending depending on the person (I, you, they, etc.) and form (singular, plural). The most essential verbs in Greek are the verbs **είμαι** 'I am' and **έχω** 'I have'.

to be		
είμαι	I am	**ee**me
είσαι	you are	**ee**se
είναι	he/she/it is	**ee**ne
είμαστε	we are	**ee**maste
είστε	you are	**ee**ste*
είναι	they are	**ee**ne

* This form is also used when addressing someone you do not know very well; it is generally referred to as the polite plural (like the French 'vous').

Note: While in English it is necessary to use the personal pronoun, i.e. we, you, etc., in order to distinguish between 'we are', 'you are', etc., in

Greek this function is carried out by the different endings of the verb itself. Thus, in Greek, 'we are' and 'they are' can be simply **είμαστε** (**ee**maste), **είναι** (**ee**ne).

to have		
έχω	I have	**e**kho
έχεις	you have	**e**khees
έχει	he/she/it has	**e**khee
έχουμε	we have	**e**khoome
έχετε	you have	**e**khete
έχουν	they have	**e**khoon

Note: As above, 'I have' can be expressed in Greek with simply the verb **έχω**; each ending is particular to a specific person.

Verbs in Greek, in the active voice, end in **-ω** (o) or **-ώ** (o). This is the ending with which they generally appear in dictionaries. Note that in everyday speech a more usual ending for **-ώ** (o) is **-άω** (ao). If a verb does not have an active voice form, in a dictionary it will appear with the ending **-μαι** (-me), e.g.

λυπάμαι (leep**a**me) to be sad or sorry

θυμάμαι (theem**a**me) to remember

In the present tense conjugation, the verb **αγαπώ**
(aghap**o**) 'to love' has typical endings for verbs
ending in **-ώ** (-o), while those ending in **-ω** (-o)
follow the pattern of **έχω** (**e**kho) above.

αγαπώ/άω (aghap**o**/**a**o)	I love
αγαπάς (aghap**a**s)	you love
αγαπά (aghap**a**)	he/she/it loves
αγαπούμε (aghap**oo**me)	we love
αγαπάτε (aghap**a**te)	you love
αγαπούν (aghap**oo**n)	they love

Negative

. . . .

In order to make a sentence negative, you just add
δεν (dhen) so that it immediately precedes the verb,
e.g.:

I don't know	**δεν ξέρω**
	dhen ks**e**ro
I have no...	**δεν έχω...**
	dhen **e**kho

Future

Similar to the technique of negating a sentence, the future tense is made by adding **θα** (tha) immediately before the verb, e.g.:

θα πάω tha pao	I shall go
δε θα πάω dhe tha pao	I shall not go

Forms of address

In Greek, there are two ways of addressing people, depending on their age, social or professional status, and how formal or informal the relationship is. For example, an older person is likely to address a much younger person in the singular (informal) form but the younger person would respond using the plural (formal) unless the two are very well acquainted. Two friends will speak to each other using the informal singular:

Τι κάνεις; (tee kanees?)	How are you?
Καλά, εσύ; (kala esee?)	Fine, and you?

But two acquaintances will address each other in a more formal way, using the plural:

Τι κάνετε; (tee k**a**nete?) How are you?

Καλά, εσείς; (kal**a**, es**ee**s?) Fine, and you?

Personal pronouns

• •

A pronoun is a word used to refer to someone or something that has been mentioned earlier, such as 'it', 'they', 'him'. There are times when a personal pronoun needs to be used in Greek, e.g. in order to establish the sex of the person or to establish the gender of the thing referred to, i.e. he, she or it.

εγώ	I	egh**o**
εσύ	you	es**ee**
αυτός	he	aft**o**s
αυτή	she	aft**ee**
αυτό	it	aft**o**
εμείς	we	em**ee**s
εσείς	you	es**ee**s
αυτοί	they (masculine)	aft**ee**
αυτές	they (feminine)	aft**e**s
αυτά	they (neuter)	aft**a**

Thus:

αυτός έχει (aft**os e**khee)   he has

αυτή έχει (aft**ee e**khee)   she has

English – Greek Dictionary

A

a (masculine **o** words)	ένας	enas
(feminine **η** words)	μία	meea
(neuter **το** words)	ένα	ena
about: *a book about Athens*	ένα βιβλίο για την Αθήνα	ena veevleeo ya teen Atheena
at about ten o'clock	περίπου στις δέκα	pereepoo stees dheka
above	πάνω από	pano apo
accident	το ατύχημα	to ateekheema
accommodation	το κατάλυμμα	to kataleema
address	η διεύθυνση	ee dheeeftheensee
admission charge	η είσοδος	ee eesodhos
adult	ο ενήλικος	o eneeleekos
advance: *in advance*	προκαταβολικά	prokatavoleeka
Aegean Sea	το Αιγαίο (πέλαγος)	to egheo (pelaghos)
aeroplane	το αεροπλάνο	to aeroplano
after	μετά	meta
afternoon	το απόγευμα	to apoyevma
again	πάλι/ξανά	palee/ksana
ago: *a week ago*	πριν μια βδομάδα	preen mya vdhomadha
air conditioning	ο κλιματισμός	o kleemateesmos
airline	η αεροπορική εταιρία	ee aeroporeekee etereea
airport	το αεροδρόμιο	to aerodhromeeo
airport bus	το λεωφορείο για/το αεροδρόμιο	to leoforeeo ya/to aerodhromeeo
air ticket	το αεροπορικό εισιτήριο	to aeroporeeko eeseeteereeo

alarm (emergency)	ο συναγερμός	o seenayermos
alarm clock	το ξυπνητήρι	to kseepneeteeree
alcohol	το αλκοόλ	to alko-ol
alcohol-free	χωρίς αλκοόλ	khorees alko-ol
alcoholic	οινοπνευματώδης	eenopnevmatodhees
all	όλος	olos
all the milk	όλο το γάλα	olo to ghala
all the time	όλον τον καιρό	olon ton kero
allergic to	αλλεργικός σε	aleryeekos se
all right (agreed)	εντάξει	endaksee
also	επίσης	epeesees
always	πάντα	panda
ambulance	το ασθενοφόρο	to asthenoforo
America	η Αμερική	ee amereekee
American	ο Αμερικανός/η Αμερικανίδα	o amereekanos/ee amereekaneedha
and	και	ke
angry	θυμωμένος	theemomenos
another	άλλος	alos
another beer	άλλη μία μπίρα	alee meea beera
answer	η απάντηση	ee apandeesee
to answer	απαντώ	apando
answerphone	ο αυτόματος τηλεφωνητής	o aftomatos teelefoneetees
antibiotics	τα αντιβιοτικά	ta andeeveeoteeka
antiseptic	το αντισηπτικό	to andeeseepteeko
apartment	το διαμέρισμα	to dheeamereesma
arm	το μπράτσο	to bratso
around	γύρω	yeero

arrivals	οι αφίξεις	ee afeeksees
to arrive	φτάνω	ftano
aspirin	η ασπιρίνη	ee aspeereenee
asthma	το άσθμα	to asthma
at	σε	se
at the (masculine, neuter)	στο	sto
at the (feminine)	στη	stee
attractive (person)	ελκυστικός	elkeesteekos
Australia	η Αυστραλία	ee afstraleea
Australian	ο Αυστραλός/η Αυστραλέζα	o afstralos/ee afstraleza
automatic	αυτόματος	aftomatos
autumn	το φθινόπωρο	to ftheenoporo
awful	φοβερός	foveros

B

baby	το μωρό	to moro
baby's bottle	το μπιμπερό	to beebero
baby seat (in car)	το παιδικό κάθισμα	to pedheeko katheesma
baby-sitter	η μπεϊμπισίτερ	ee babysitter
baby wipes	τα υγρά μαντηλάκια για μωρά	ta eeghra mandeelakya ya mora
back (of a person)	η πλάτη	ee platee
bad (of food)	χαλασμένος	khalasmenos
(of weather)	κακός	kakos
bag (small)	η τσάντα	ee tsanda
(suitcase)	η βαλίτσα	ee valeetsa

baggage	οι αποσκευές	ee aposkeves
bank	η τράπεζα	ee trapeza
banknote	το χαρτονόμισμα	to khartonomeesma
bar	το μπαρ	to bar
bath (tub)	το μπάνιο	to banyo
to take a bath	κάνω μπάνιο	kano banyo
bathroom	το μπάνιο	to banyo
battery	η μπαταρία	ee batareea
beach	η πλαζ/η παραλία	ee plaz/ee paraleea
beautiful	όμορφος	omorfos
because	επειδή	epeedhee
bed	το κρεβάτι	to krevatee
double bed	διπλό κρεβάτι	dheeplo krevatee
single bed	μονό κρεβάτι	mono krevatee
twin beds	δύο μονά κρεβάτια	dheeo mona krevatya
bedroom	η κρεβατοκάμαρα	ee krevatokamara
beer	η μπύρα	ee beera
before (time)	πριν (από)	preen (apo)
(place)	μπροστά από	brosta apo
to begin	αρχίζω	arkheezo
behind	πίσω από	peeso apo
to believe	πιστεύω	peestevo
below	κάτω από	kato apo
beside	δίπλα	dheepla
best	ο καλύτερος	o kaleeteros
better (than)	καλύτερος (από)	kaleeteros (apo)
between	μεταξύ	metaksee
bicycle	το ποδήλατο	to podheelato

big	μεγάλος	meghalos
bigger	μεγαλύτερος	meghaleeteros
bill	ο λογαριασμός	o logharyasmos
birthday	τα γενέθλια	ta yenethleea
happy birthday!	χρόνια πολλά	khronya pola
biscuit	το μπισκότο	to beeskoto
bit: *a bit (of)*	λίγο	leegho
bite (insect)	το τσίμπημα	to tseebeema
bitten: *I have been bitten*	με δάγκωσε	me dhangkose
bitter	πικρός	peekros
black	μαύρος	mavros
blocked (pipe)	βουλωμένος	voolomenos
(nose)	κλειστή	kleestee
blood pressure	η πίεση αίματος	ee peeyesee ematos
blouse	η μπλούζα	ee blooza
blow-dry	στέγνωμα	steghnoma
blue	γαλάζιος/μπλε	ghalazyos/ble
boat (small)	η βάρκα	ee varka
(ship)	το πλοίο	to pleeo
to boil	βράζω	vrazo
book	το βιβλίο	to veevleeo
to book (room, tickets)	κλείνω	kleeno
booking: *to make a booking*	κλείνω θέση	kleeno thesee
booking office (railways, airlines, etc.)	το εκδοτήριο	to ekdhoteereeo
(theatre)	το ταμείο	to tameeo

bookshop	το βιβλιοπωλείο	to veevleeopoleeo
boots	οι μπότες	ee botes
boring	βαρετός	varetos
bottle	το μπουκάλι	to bookalee
box office	το ταμείο	to tameeo
boy	το αγόρι	to aghoree
boyfriend	ο φίλος	o feelos
to brake	φρενάρω	frenaro
brakes	τα φρένα	ta frena
bread	το ψωμί	to psomee
(wholemeal)	ψωμί ολικής αλέσεως	psomee oleekees aleseos
to break	σπάζω	spazo
breakfast	το πρωινό	to proeeno
breast	το στήθος	to steethos
to breathe	αναπνέω	anapneo
bride	η νύφη	ee neefee
bridegroom	ο γαμπρός	o ghambros
to bring	φέρνω	ferno
Britain	η Βρετανία	ee vretaneea
British	ο Βρετανός/η Βρετανίδα	o vretanos/ee vretaneedha
broken	σπασμένος	spasmenos
broken down	χαλασμένος	khalasmenos
brother	ο αδελφός	o adhelfos
brown	καφέ	kafe
bulb (light)	ο γλόμπος	o ghlobos
bureau de change (bank)	ξένο συνάλλαγμα	kseno seenalaghma

bus	το λεωφορείο	to leoforeeo
business	η δουλειά	ee dhoolya
business centre	το εμπορικό κέντρο	to emboreeko kendro
bus station	ο σταθμός του λεωφορείου	o stathmos too leoforeeoo
bus stop	η στάση του λεωφορείου	ee stasee too leoforeeoo
bus terminal	το τέρμα του λεωφορείου	to terma too leoforeeoo
busy	απασχολημένος	apaskholeemenos
but	αλλά	ala
to buy	αγοράζω	aghorazo

C

cab	το ταξί	to taksee
café	το καφενείο	to kafeneeo
cake	το γλύκισμα	to ghleekeesma
call (telephone)	η κλήση	ee kleesee
long-distance call	η υπεραστική κλήση	ee eeperasteekee kleesee
to call	φωνάζω	fonazo
calm	ήσυχος	eeseekhos
camera	η φωτογραφική μηχανή	ee fotoghrafeekee meekhanee
to camp	κατασκηνώνω	kataskeenono
campsite	το κάμπινγκ	to camping
can: *I can*	μπορώ	boro
you can	μπορείς	borees
he can	μπορεί	boree

we can	μπορούμε	boroome
can (of food)	η κονσέρβα	ee konserva
Canada	ο Καναδάς	o kanadhas
Canadian	ο Καναδός/η Καναδή	o Kanadhos/ee Kanadhee
to cancel	ακυρώνω	akeerono
car	το αυτοκίνητο	to aftokeeneeto
car ferry	το φεριμπότ	to fereebot
car keys	τα κλειδιά αυτοκινήτου	ta kleedhya aftokeeneetoo
car park	το πάρκινγκ	to parking
card	η κάρτα	ee karta
careful	προσεκτικός	prosekteekos
carriage (railway)	το βαγόνι	to vaghonee
to carry	κουβαλώ	koovalo
to cash (cheque)	εξαργυρώνω	eksaryeerono
cash	τα μετρητά	ta metreeta
cash desk	το ταμείο	to tameeo
cash dispenser	το ATM	to ey tee em
castle	το κάστρο	to kastro
casualty department	τμήμα για επείγοντα περιστατικά	tmeema ya epeeghonda pereestateeka
cat	η γάτα	ee ghata
catalogue	ο κατάλογος	o kataloghos
to catch	πιάνω	pyano
(bus, train, etc.)	παίρνω	perno
Catholic	καθολικός	katholikos
cents (euro)	λεπτά	lepta
centimetre	το εκατοστό	to ekatosto

central	κεντρικός	kendreekos
centre	το κέντρο	to kendro
century	ο αιώνας	o eonas
certificate	το πιστοποιητικό	to peestopeeeeteeko
chain	η αλυσίδα	ee aleeseedha
chair	η καρέκλα	ee karekla
champagne	η σαμπάνια	ee sambanya
change	η αλλαγή	ee alaghee
(money)	τα ρέστα	ta resta
to change	αλλάζω	alazo
charge (price)	η τιμή	ee teemee
charge (electric)	η φόρτιση	ee forteesee
I've run out of charge	έμεινα από μπαταρία	emeena apo batareea
cheap	φτηνός	fteenos
to check	ελέγχω	elenkho
to check in	περνώ από τον έλεγχο εισιτηρίων	perno apo ton elenkho eeseeteereeon
cheers!	γεια μας!	ya mas!
cheese	το τυρί	to teeree
chemist's	το φαρμακείο	to farmakeeo
cheque	η επιταγή	ee epeetaghee
cheque card	η κάρτα επιταγών	ee karta epeetaghon
child	το παιδί	to pedhee
children	τα παιδιά	ta pedhya
chips	πατάτες τηγανητές	patates teeghaneetes
chocolate	η σοκολάτα	ee sokolata
Christmas	τα Χριστούγεννα	ta khreestooyena
merry Christmas!	καλά Χριστούγεννα	kala khreestooyena

church	η εκκλησία	ee ekleeseea
cigarette	το τσιγάρο	to tseegharo
cinema	ο κινηματογράφος	o keeneematoghrafos
city	η πόλη	ee polee
clean	καθαρός	katharos
to clean	καθαρίζω	kathareezo
client	ο πελάτης/η πελάτισσα	o pelatees/ee pelateesa
climbing	η ορειβασία	ee oreevaseea
clock	το ρολόι	to roloee
to close	κλείνω	kleeno
close *adj* (near)	κοντινός	kondeenos
(weather)	αποπνιχτικός	apopneekhteekos
closed	κλειστός	kleestos
clothes	τα ρούχα	ta rookha
cloudy	συννεφιασμένος	seenefyasmenos
coach (railway)	το βαγόνι	to vaghonee
(bus)	το πούλμαν	to poolman
coach station	ο σταθμός λεωφορείων	o stathmos leoforeeon
coast	η ακτή	ee aktee
coat	το παλτό	to palto
coffee	ο καφές	o kafes
black coffee	σκέτος καφές	sketos kafes
white coffee	καφές με γάλα	kafes me ghala
cold	κρύος	kreeos
I have a cold	είμαι κρυωμένος	eeme kreeomenos
I'm cold	κρυώνω	kreeono
colour	το χρώμα	to khroma

to come	έρχομαι	erkhome
to come back	γυρίζω	yeereezo
to come in	μπαίνω	beno
comfortable	αναπαυτικός	anapafteekos
company (firm)	η εταιρία	ee etereea
compartment (train)	το βαγόνι	to vaghonee
to complain	παραπονούμαι	paraponoome
computer	το κομπιούτερ	to kompyooter
concert	η συναυλία	ee seenavleea
condom	το προφυλακτικό	to profeelakteeko
to confirm	επιβεβαιώνω	epeeveveono
congratulations!	συγχαρητήρια	seenkhareeteereea
connection (trains, etc.)	η σύνδεση	ee seendhesee
consulate	το προξενείο	to prokseneeo
to contact	έρχομαι σε επαφή	erkhome se epafee
contact lenses	οι φακοί	ee fakee epafees
contraceptives	τα αντισυλληπτικά	ta andeeseeleepteeka
contract	το συμβόλαιο	to seemvoleo
to cook	μαγειρεύω	magheerevo
cooker	η κουζίνα	ee koozeena
cool	δροσερός	dhroseros
copy noun	το αντίγραφο	to andeeghrafo
to copy (photocopy)	φωτοτυπώ	fototeepo
corner	η γωνία	ee ghoneea
cosmetics	τα καλλυντικά	ta kaleendeeka
to cost	κοστίζω	kosteezo

how much does it cost?	πόσο κάνει;	poso kanee;
cough	ο βήχας	o veekhas
country	η χώρα	ee khora
(not town)	η εξοχή	ee eksokhee
couple (two people)	το ζευγάρι	to zevgharee
course (meal)	το πιάτο	to pyato
cousin	ο εξάδελφος/η εξαδέλφη	o eksadhelfos/ee eksadhelfee
cover charge	το κουβέρ	to koover
to crash	συγκρούομαι	seengkrooome
crash	η σύγκρουση	ee seenkgroosee
crash helmet	το κράνος	to kranos
credit (on mobile phone)	οι μονάδες	ee monadhes
credit card	η πιστωτική κάρτα	ee peestoteekee karta
to cross	διασχίζω	dheeaskheezo
crowded	γεμάτος	yematos
cruise	η κρουαζιέρα	ee krooazyera
cup	το φλυτζάνι	to fleedzanee
current (electric)	το ρεύμα	to revma
customer	ο πελάτης	o pelatees
to cut	κόβω	kovo
to cycle	ποδηλατώ	podheelato
cystitis	η κυστίτιδα	ee keesteeteedha

D

daily	ημερήσιος	eemereeseeos
dairy products	τα γαλακτοκομικά προϊόντα	ta ghalaktokomeeka proeeonda

damage	η ζημιά	ee zeemya
damp	υγρός	eeghros
dance	ο χορός	o khoros
to dance	χορεύω	khorevo
danger	ο κίνδυνος	o keendheenos
dangerous	επικίνδυνος	epeekeendheenos
dark (colour)	σκούρο	skooro
date	η ημερομηνία	ee eemeromeeneea
date of birth	η ημερομηνία γεννήσεως	ee eemeromeeneea yeneeseos
daughter	η κόρη	ee koree
day	η μέρα	ee mera
dead	νεκρός	nekros
dear	αγαπητός	aghapeetos
(expensive)	ακριβός	akreevos
debit card	η χρεωστική κάρτα	ee khreosteekee karta
decaffeinated	χωρίς καφεΐνη	khorees kafe-eenee
deck chair	η ξαπλώστρα	ee ksaplostra
deep	βαθύς	vathees
delay	η καθυστέρηση	ee katheestereesee
delayed	καθυστερημένος	katheestereemenos
delicious	νόστιμος	nosteemos
dentist	ο/η οδοντίατρος	o/ee odhondeeatros
deodorant	το αποσμητικό	to aposmeeteeko
department store	το πολυκατά-στημα	to poleekatasteema
departure	η αναχώρηση	ee anakhoreesee
diabetic	διαβητικός	dheeaveeteekos
to dial	παίρνω αριθμό	perno areethmo

dialling code	ο τηλεφωνικός κώδικας	o teelefoneekos kodheekas
diet	η δίαιτα	ee dhee-eta
I'm on a diet	κάνω δίαιτα	kano dhee-eta
different	διαφορετικός	dheeaforeteekos
difficult	δύσκολος	dheeskolos
digital camera	η ψηφιακή φωτογραφική μηχανή	ee pseefeeakee fotoghrafeekee meekhanee
dining room	η τραπεζαρία	ee trapezareea
dinner	το δείπνο	to dheepno
direct	άμεσος	amesos
directory (telephone)	ο τηλεφωνικός κατάλογος	o teelefoneekos kataloghos
dirty	βρόμικος	vromeekos
disabled	ανάπηρος	anapeeros
discount	η έκπτωση	ee ekptosee
divorced	χωρισμένος/ χωρισμένη	khoreesmenos/ khoreesmenee
dizzy	ζαλισμένος	zaleesmenos
to do: I do	κάνω	kano
you do	κάνεις	kanees
doctor	ο/η γιατρός	o/ee yatros
documents	τα έγγραφα	ta engrafa
dog	το σκυλί	to skeelee
dollar	το δολάριο	to dholareeo
door	η πόρτα	ee porta
double	διπλός	dheeplos
double bed	το διπλό κρεββάτι	to dheeplo krevatee

double room	το δίκλινο δωμάτιο	to dheekleeno dhomateeo
down: to go down	κατεβαίνω	kateveno
downstairs	κάτω	kato
dress	το φόρεμα	to forema
to dress	ντύνομαι	deenome
drink noun	το ποτό	to poto
to have a drink	παίρνω ένα ποτό	perno ena poto
to drink	πίνω	peeno
drinking water	το πόσιμο νερό	to poseemo nero
to drive	οδηγώ	odheegho
driver	ο οδηγός	o odheeghos
driving licence	η άδεια οδήγησης	ee adheea odheegheesees
to drown	πνίγομαι	pneeghome
drug (illegal)	το ναρκωτικό	to narkoteeko
(medicine)	το φάρμακο	to farmako
drunk	μεθυσμένος	metheesmenos
dry adj	στεγνός	steghnos
to dry	στεγνώνω	steghnono
dry-cleaners	το καθαριστήριο	to kathareesteereeo
during	κατά τη διάρκεια	kata tee dheearkeea

E

each	κάθε	kathe
ear	το αυτί	to aftee
earache: I have earache	με πονάει το αυτί μου	me ponaee to aftee moo
earlier	νωρίτερα	noreetera

early	νωρίς	norees
east	η ανατολή	ee anatolee
Easter	το Πάσχα	to paskha
easy	εύκολος	efkolos
to eat	τρώω	troo
electronic	ηλεκτρονικός/ή/ό	eelektroneekos/ee/o
e-mail	το e-mail	to e-mail
e-mail address	η διεύθυνση e-mail	ee dhee-eftheensee e-mail
embassy	η πρεσβεία	ee presveea
emergency: *it's an emergency*	είναι επείγον περιστατικό	eene epeeghon pereestateeko
empty	άδειος	adheeos
end	το τέλος	to telos
engaged (to marry)	αρραβωνια-σμένος/η	aravonyasmenos/ee
engine	η μηχανή	ee meekhanee
England	η Αγγλία	ee angleea
English (thing)	αγγλικός	angleekos
Englishman/woman	ο Άγγλος/η Αγγλίδα	o anglos/ee angleedha
to enjoy oneself	διασκεδάζω	dhyaskedhazo
enough	αρκετά	arketa
enough bread	αρκετό ψωμί	arketo psomee
enquiry desk/office	το γραφείο πληροφοριών	to ghrafeeo pleeroforeeon
to enter	μπαίνω	beno
entrance	η είσοδος	ee eesodhos
entrance fee	η τιμή εισόδου	ee teemee eesodhoo
essential	απαραίτητος	apareeteetos

euro	ευρώ	evro
Europe	η Ευρώπη	ee evropee
evening	το βράδυ	to vradhee
this evening	απόψε	apopse
in the evening	το βράδυ	to vradhee
every	κάθε	kathe
everyone	όλοι	olee
everything	όλα	ola
excellent	εξαιρετικός	eksereteekos
except	εκτός από	ektos apo
exchange rate	η τιμή του συναλλάγματος	ee teemee too seenalaghmatos
excuse me	με συγχωρείτε	me seeghkhoreete
exit	η έξοδος	ee eksodhos
expensive	ακριβός	akreevos
extra: *it costs extra*	κοστίζει επιπλέον	kosteezee epeepleon
extra money	περισσότερα χρήματα	pereesotera khreemata
eyes	τα μάτια	ta matya

F

face	το πρόσωπο	to prosopo
facilities	οι ευκολίες	ee efkoleeyes
to faint	λιποθυμώ	leepotheemo
to fall	πέφτω	pefto
he/she has fallen	έπεσε	epese
family	η οικογένεια	ee eekoyeneea
fan (electric)	ο ανεμιστήρας	o anemeesteeras

far	μακριά	makreea
fare (bus, train)	το εισιτήριο	to eeseeteereeo
fast	γρήγορα	ghreeghora
father	ο πατέρας	o pateras
fault (mistake)	το λάθος	to lathos
it is not my fault	δε φταίω εγώ	dhe fteo egho
fax	το φαξ	fax
to feel	αισθάνομαι	esthanome
I feel sick	θέλω να κάνω εμετό	thelo na kano emeto
female	θηλυκός	theeleekos
ferry	το φεριμπότ	to fereebot
to fetch	φέρνω	ferno
fever	ο πυρετός	o peeretos
fiancé(e)	ο αρραβωνιαστικός/η αρραβωνιαστικιά	o aravonyasteekos/ee aravonyasteekya
to fill	γεμίζω	yemeezo
fill it up! (car)	γεμίστε το	yemeeste to
fillet	το φιλέτο	to feeleto
film (for camera)	το φιλμ	to feelm
(in cinema)	η ταινία	ee teneea
to finish	τελειώνω	teleeono
fire (heater)	η θερμάστρα	ee thermastra
fire!	φωτιά!	fotya!
fire brigade	η πυροσβεστική	ee peerosvesteekee
fire extinguisher	ο πυροσβεστήρας	o peerosvesteeras
first	πρώτος	protos
first aid	οι πρώτες βοήθειες	ee protes voeetheeyes

first class (seat, etc.)	η πρώτη θέση	ee protee thesee
first name	το όνομα	to onoma
fish	το ψάρι	to psaree
to fish	ψαρεύω	psarevo
fit (healthy)	υγιής	eeyees
to fix	φτιάχνω	ftyakhno
(arrange)	κανονίζω	kanoneezo
fizzy (drink)	αεριούχο	aeryookho
flat (apartment)	το διαμέρισμα	to dheeamereesma
flight	η πτήση	ee pteesee
floor	το πάτωμα	to patoma
(storey)	ο όροφος	o orofos
flower	το λουλούδι	to looloodhee
flu	η γρίππη	ee ghreepee
to fly	πετώ	peto
food	το φαγητό	to fayeeto
food poisoning	η τροφική δηλητηρίαση	ee trofeekee dhee-leeteereeasee
foot	το πόδι	to podhee
football	το ποδόσφαιρο	to podhosfero
for	για	ya
foreign	ξένος	ksenos
to forget	ξεχνώ	ksekhno
fork	το πηρούνι	to peeroonee
(in road)	η διακλάδωση	ee dheeakladhosee
fracture (of bone)	το κάταγμα	to kataghma
France	η Γαλλία	ee ghaleea
free	ελεύθερος	eleftheros
(costing nothing)	δωρεάν	dhorean

French (thing)	γαλλικός	ghaleekos
frequent	συχνός	seekhnos
fresh	φρέσκος	freskos
fried	τηγανητός	teeghaneetos
friend	ο φίλος/η φίλη	o feelos/ee feelee
from	από	apo
front (part)	το μπροστινό (μέρος)	to brosteeno (meros)
in front	μπροστά	brosta
fruit	τα φρούτα	ta froota
fruit juice	ο χυμός φρούτων	o kheemos frooton
full	γεμάτος	yematos
full board	(η) πλήρης διατροφή	(ee) pleerees dheeatrofee
funny	αστείος	asteeos

G

gallery (art)	η πινακοθήκη	ee peenakotheekee
game	το παιγνίδι	to peghneedhee
(to eat)	το κυνήγι	to keeneeghee
garage (for parking car)	το γκαράζ	to garaz
garden	ο κήπος	o keepos
gate (at airport)	η έξοδος	ee eksodhos
gents (toilet)	ανδρών	andhron
genuine	γνήσιος	ghneeseeos
to get	παίρνω	perno
(fetch)	φέρνω	ferno
to get in (car, etc.)	μπαίνω	beno

to get off (from bus)	κατεβαίνω από	kateveno apo
to get on (bus)	ανεβαίνω στο (λεωφορείο)	aneveno sto (leoforeeo)
gift	το δώρο	to dhoro
girl	το κορίτσι	to koreetsee
girlfriend	η φίλη/η φιλενάδα	ee feelee/ee feelenadha
to give	δίνω	dheeno
glass (to drink from)	το ποτήρι	to poteeree
a glass of water	ένα ποτήρι νερό	ena poteeree nero
glasses (spectacles)	τα γυαλιά	ta yalya
to go	πηγαίνω	peegheno
I go/I am going	πηγαίνω	peegheno
you go/you are going	πηγαίνεις	peeghenees
we go/we are going	πηγαίνουμε	peeghenoome
to go back	γυρίζω πίσω	yeereezo peeso
to go in	μπαίνω	beno
to go out	βγαίνω	vyeno
gold	ο χρυσός	o khreesos
(made of gold)	χρυσός	khreesos
good	καλός	kalos
good afternoon	χαίρετε	kherete
goodbye	αντίο	adeeo
good day	καλημέρα	kaleemera
good evening	καλησπέρα	kaleespera
good morning	καλημέρα	kaleemera
good night	καληνύχτα	kaleeneekhta
grandfather	ο παππούς	o papoos

grandmother	η γιαγιά	ee yaya
grapes	τα σταφύλια	ta stafeelya
great	μεγάλος	meghalos
Greece	η Ελλάδα	ee eladha
Greek (person)	ο Έλληνας/η Ελληνίδα	o eleenas/ee eleeneedha
Greek adj	ελληνικός	eleeneekos
green	πράσινος	praseenos
grey	γκρίζος	greezos
grocer's	το μπακάλικο	to bakaleeko
	το παντοπωλείο	to pandopoleeo
group	η ομάδα	ee omadha
guest	ο φιλοξενούμενος	o feeloksenoomenos
guide	ο/η ξεναγός	o/ee ksenaghos
guidebook	ο οδηγός	o odheeghos

H

hair	τα μαλλιά	ta malya
hairdresser	ο κομμωτής/η κομμώτρια	o komotees/ee komotreea
half	το μισό	to meeso
half an hour	μισή ώρα	meesee ora
half board	(η) ημιδιατροφή	(ee) eemeedhee- atrofee
half price	μισή τιμή	meesee teemee
hand	το χέρι	to kheree
handbag	η τσάντα	ee tsanda
handicapped	ανάπηρος	anapeeros
handkerchief	το μαντήλι	to mandeelee

(tissue)	το χαρτομάντηλο	to khartomandeelo
hand luggage	η χειραποσκευή	ee kheeraposkevee
hand-made	χειροποίητος	kheeropee-eetos
to happen	συμβαίνω	seemveno
what happened?	τι συνέβη;	tee seenevee?
happy	χαρούμενος	kharoomenos
hard (difficult)	δύσκολος	dheeskolos
hat	το καπέλο	to kapelo
he	αυτός	aftos
head	το κεφάλι	to kefalee
headache: *I have a headache*	έχω πονοκέφαλο	ekho ponokefalo
health	η υγεία	ee eegheea
to hear	ακούω	akoo-o
heart	η καρδιά	ee kardhya
heating	η θέρμανση	ee thermansee
heavy	βαρύς	varees
hello	γεια σας	ya sas
to help	βοηθώ	voeetho
help!	βοήθεια	voeetheea
here	εδώ	edho
to hire	νοικιάζω	neekyazo
to hold	κρατώ	krato
hold-up	η καθυστέρηση	ee katheestereesee
holidays	οι διακοπές	ee dheeakopes
home	το σπίτι	to speetee
at home	στο σπίτι	sto speetee
to hope	ελπίζω	elpeezo
hospital	το νοσοκομείο	to nosokomeeo

...ot	ζεστός	zestos
I'm hot	ζεσταίνομαι	zestenome
...t's hot	έχει ζέστη	ekhee zestee
...ot water	το ζεστό νερό	to zesto nero
...otel	το ξενοδοχείο	to ksenodhokheeo
...our	η ώρα	ee ora
...ouse	το σπίτι	to speetee
...ouse wine	το κρασί χύμα	to krasee kheema
...ow	πώς	pos
...ow long?	πόση ώρα;	posee ora?
...ow much?	πόσο;	poso?
...ow many?	πόσα;	posa?
...ow are you?	πώς είστε;	pos eeste?
...ungry: I'm hungry	πεινώ	peeno
...o hurry: I'm in a hurry	βιάζομαι	vyazome
...o hurt: that hurts	με πονάει	me ponaee
...usband	ο σύζυγος	o seezeeghos

	εγώ	egho
...ce	ο πάγος	o paghos
...ce cream/ice olly	το παγωτό	to paghoto
...f	αν	an
...ll	άρρωστος	arostos
...mmediately	αμέσως	amesos
...mpossible	αδύνατο	adheenato

English – Greek

in (inside)	μέσα	mesa
(into)	σε	se
(with countries, towns)	στο/στη/στο	sto/stee/sto
infectious	μεταδοτικός	metadhoteekos
information	οι πληροφορίες	ee pleeroforeeyes
injured	τραυματι-σμένος	travmateesmenos
insect	το έντομο	to endomo
inside (interior)	το εσωτερικό	to esotereeko
inside the car	μέσα στο αυτοκίνητο	mesa sto aftokeeneeto
it's inside	είναι μέσα	eene mesa
insurance	η ασφάλεια	ee asfaleea
insured	ασφαλισμένος	asfaleesmenos
interesting	ενδιαφέρων	endheeaferon
international	διεθνής	dhee-ethnees
to invite	προσκαλώ	proskalo
Ireland	η Ιρλανδία	ee eerlandheea
Irish (person)	ο Ιρλανδός/η Ιρλανδή	o eerlandhos/ee eerlandhee
iron (for clothes)	το σίδερο	to seedhero
island	το νησί	to neesee
it	το	to
Italy	η Ιταλία	ee eetaleea
itch	η φαγούρα	ee faghoora

J

jacket	το μπουφάν	to boofan
jam	η μαρμελάδα	ee marmeladha

jar	το βάζο	to vazo
jeans	το τζιν	to jean
jeweller's	το κοσμηματο-πωλείο	to kosmeemato-poleeo
jewellery	τα κοσμήματα	ta kosmeemata
job	η δουλειά	ee dhoolya
joke	το αστείο	to asteeo
journey	το ταξίδι	to takseedhee
juice	ο χυμός	o kheemos
just: *just two*	μόνο δύο	mono dheeo
I've just arrived	μόλις έφτασα	molees eftasa

K

to keep	κρατώ	krato
key	το κλειδί	to kleedhee
kilo	το κιλό	to keelo
kilometre	το χιλιόμετρο	to kheelyometro
kind (sort)	το είδος	to eedhos
kind *adj*	ευγενικός	evgheneekos
kiosk	το περίπτερο	to pereeptero
kitchen	η κουζίνα	ee koozeena
knife	το μαχαίρι	to makheree
to knock down (by car)	χτυπώ με αυτοκίνητο	khteepo me aftokeeneeto

L

ladies (toilet)	γυναικών	yeenekon
lady	η κυρία	ee keereea
lager	η μπύρα	ee beera

lamb	το αρνάκι	to arnakee
lamp	η λάμπα	ee lamba
to land (plane)	προσγειώνω	prosgheeono
language	η γλώσσα	ee ghlosa
large	μεγάλος	meghalos
last	τελευταίος	telefteos
late (in the day)	αργά	argha
I am late (for an appointment)	έχω αργήσει	ekho argheesee
later	αργότερα	arghotera
lavatory	η τουαλέτα	ee tooaleta
lazy	τεμπέλης	tembelees
to learn	μαθαίνω	matheno
leather	το δέρμα	to dherma
to leave (go away)	φεύγω	fevgho
left: *(on/to the) left*	αριστερά	areestera
left-luggage (office)	η φύλαξη αποσκευών	ee feelaksee aposkevon
leg	το πόδι	to podhee
lemon	το λεμόνι	to lemonee
lemonade	η λεμονάδα	ee lemonadha
lens	ο φακός	o fakos
less: *less milk*	λιγότερο γάλα	leeghotero ghala
lesson	το μάθημα	to matheema
to let (allow)	επιτρέπω	epeetrepo
(hire out)	νοικιάζω	neekyazo
letter	το γράμμα	to ghrama
licence	η άδεια	ee adheea

to lie down	ξαπλώνω	ksaplono
lift	το ασανσέρ	to asanser
light	το φως	to fos
to like : I like	μου αρέσει	moo aresee
line	η γραμμή	ee ghramee
to listen	ακούω	akoo-o
litre	το λίτρο	to leetro
little	μικρός	meekros
a little	λίγο	leegho
to live	μένω	meno
he lives in London	μένει στο Λονδίνο	menee sto londheeno
lock	η κλειδαριά	ee kleedharya
to lock	κλειδώνω	kleedhono
I'm locked out	κλειδώθηκα έξω	kleedhotheeka ekso
London	το Λονδίνο	to londheeno
long	μακρύς	makrees
to look after	φροντίζω	frondeezo
to look at	κοιτάζω	keetazo
to lose	χάνω	khano
lost	χαμένος	khamenos
I've lost my wallet	έχασα το πορτοφόλι μου	ekhasa to portofolee moo
I am lost	χάθηκα	khatheeka
lost-property office	το γραφείο απολεσθέντων αντικειμένων	to ghrafeeo apolesthendon andeekeemenon
lot: a lot (of)	πολύς	polees
loud	δυνατός	dheenatos
to love	αγαπώ	aghapo

low	χαμηλός	khameelos
luggage	οι αποσκευές	ee aposkeves
lunch	το μεσημεριανό	to meseemeryano

M

machine	η μηχανή	ee meekhanee
mad	τρελός	trelos
magazine	το περιοδικό	to pereeodheeko
main course (of meal)	το κύριο πιάτο	to keereeo pyato
to make	κάνω	kano
make-up	το μακιγιάζ	to makeeyaz
male	αρσενικός	arseneekos
man	ο άντρας	o andras
manager	ο διαχειριστής	o dheeakheereestees
many	πολλοί	polee
many people	πολλοί άνθρωποι	polee anthropee
map	ο χάρτης	o khartees
market	η αγορά	ee aghora
married	παντρεμένος	pandremenos
material	το υλικό	to eeleeko
matter: *it doesn't matter*	δεν πειράζει	dhen peerazee
what's the matter with you?	τι έχεις;	tee ekhees?
meal	το γεύμα	to yevma
meat	το κρέας	to kreas
medicine (drug)	το φάρμακο	to farmako
Mediterranean	η Μεσόγειος	ee mesoyeeos

to meet	συναντώ	seenando
meeting	η συνάντηση	ee seenandeesee
melon	το πεπόνι	to peponee
(watermelon)	το καρπούζι	to karpoozee
men	οι άντρες	ee andres
menu	ο κατάλογος/το μενού	o kataloghos/to menoo
message	το μήνυμα	to meeneema
metre	το μέτρο	to metro
midday	το μεσημέρι	to meseemeree
midnight	τα μεσάνυχτα	ta mesaneekhta
milk	το γάλα	to ghala
millimetre	το χιλιοστόμετρο	to kheelyostometro
to mind: *do you mind if...?*	σας ενοχλεί αν...;	sas enokhlee an...?
minute	το λεπτό	to lepto
to miss (train, etc.)	χάνω	khano
Miss	η δεσποινίς	ee dhespeenees
missing	χαμένος	khamenos
he's missing	λείπει/αγνοείται	leepee/agnoeete
mistake	το λάθος	to lathos
mobile (phone)	το κινητό (τηλέφωνο)	to keeneeto (teelefono)
mobile number	ο αριθμός κινητού	o areethmos keeneetoo
money	τα χρήματα/τα λεφτά	ta khreemata/ta lefta
month	ο μήνας	o meenas
more	περισσότερο	pereesotero
more bread	κι άλλο ψωμί	kee alo psomee

185

morning	το πρωί	to proee
most	το περισσότερο	to pereesotero
mother	η μητέρα	ee meetera
motor	η μηχανή	ee meekhanee
motorbike	η μοτοσικλέτα	ee motoseekleta
motorway	ο αυτοκινητό-δρομος	o aftokeeneeto-dhromos
mouth	το στόμα	to stoma
to move	κινούμαι	keenoome
Mr	Κύριος	keereeos
Mrs	Κυρία	keereea
much	πολύς	polees
too much	πάρα πολύ	para polee
very much	πάρα πολύ	para polee
museum	το μουσείο	to mooseeo
music	η μουσική	ee mooseekee
must: *I must go*	πρέπει να πάω	prepee na pao
you must go	πρέπει να πας	prepee na pas
he/she must go	πρέπει να πάει	prepee na paee
we must go	πρέπει να πάμε	prepee na pame

N

name	το όνομα	to onoma
narrow	στενός	stenos
nationality	η υπηκοότητα	ee eepeekooteeta
near	κοντά	konda
necessary	απαραίτητος	apareteetos
to need: *I need...*	χρειάζομαι...	khreeazome...

never	ποτέ	pote
new	καινούριος	kenooryos
news (TV, radio)	οι ειδήσεις	ee eedheesees
newspaper	η εφημερίδα	ee efeemereedha
New Year: *happy New Year!*	Καλή Χρονιά!	kalee khronya!
New Zealand	η Νέα Ζηλανδία	ee nea zeelandheea
next	επόμενος	epomenos
nice (thing)	ωραίος	oreos
(person)	καλός	kalos
night	η νύχτα	ee neekhta
no	όχι	okhee
nobody	κανένας	kanenas
noise	ο θόρυβος	o thoreevos
non-alcoholic	μη οινοπνευματώδης	mee eenopnevmatodhees
none	κανένα	kanena
non-smoking	μη καπνίζοντες	mee kapneezondes
north	ο βορράς	o voras
nose	η μύτη	ee meetee
not	μη/δεν	mee/dhen
I am not	δεν είμαι	dhen eeme
do not stop	μη σταματάς	mee stamatas
nothing	τίποτα	teepota
now	τώρα	tora
number	ο αριθμός	o areethmos

off (light, machine, etc.)	σβηστός	sveestos
it's off (rotten)	είναι χαλασμένο	eene khalasmeno
office	το γραφείο	to ghrafeeo
often	συχνά	seekhna
OK	εντάξει	endaksee
old (person)	ηλικιωμένος	eeleekyomenos
(thing)	παλιός	palyos
how old are you?	πόσων χρονών είστε;	poson khronon eeste?
on (on top of)	πάνω	pano
(light, TV)	ανοιχτός	aneekhtos
on the table	(πάνω) στο τραπέζι	(pano) sto trapezee
once	μία φορά	meea fora
only	μόνο	mono
open adj	ανοικτός	aneektos
to open	ανοίγω	aneegho
opposite	απέναντι	apenandee
or	ή	ee
to order	παραγγέλλω	parangelo
Orthodox (religion)	ορθόδοξος	orthodhoksos
other	άλλος	alos
out (light, etc.)	σβησμένος	sveesmenos
he's out	λείπει	leepee
outside	έξω	ekso
over	πάνω από	pano apo
over there	εκεί πέρα	ekee pera
to owe: *you owe me*	μου χρωστάς	moo khrostas

package tour	η οργανωμένη εκδρομή	ee orghanomenee ekdhromee
paid	πληρωμένος	pleeromenos
pain	ο πόνος	o ponos
painful	οδυνηρός	odheeneeros
it's painful	πονάει	ponaee
painting	ο πίνακας	o peenakas
pair	το ζευγάρι	to zevgharee
pan	η κατσαρόλα	ee katsarola
paper	το χαρτί	to khartee
parcel	το δέμα	to dhema
pardon	παρακαλώ	parakalo
I beg your pardon	με συγχωρείτε	me seegkhoreete
parents	οι γονείς	o ghonees
park noun	το πάρκο	to parko
to park (in car)	παρκάρω	parkaro
part	το μέρος	to meros
passenger	ο επιβάτης	o epeevatees
passport control	ο έλεγχος διαβατηρίων	o elengkhos dheeavateereeon
pasta	τα ζυμαρικά	ta zeemareeka
to pay	πληρώνω	pleerono
payment	η πληρωμή	ee pleeromee
pen	το στυλό	to steelo
pensioner	ο/η συνταξιούχος	o/ee seendaksyookhos
pepper (spice)	το πιπέρι	to peeperee
(vegetable)	η πιπεριά	ee peeperya

189

per: *per hour*	την ώρα	teen ora
perfect	τέλειος	teleeos
performance	η παράσταση	ee parastasee
perhaps	ίσως	eesos
person	το άτομο	to atomo
petrol	η βενζίνη	ee venzeenee
petrol station	το βενζινάδικο/το πρατήριο βενζίνης	to venzeenadheeko/ to prateereeo venzeenees
pharmacist	ο φαρμακοποιός	o farmakopeeos
phonecard	η τηλεκάρτα	ee teelekarta
photocopy	η φωτοτυπία	ee fototeepeea
photograph	η φωτογραφία	ee fotoghrafeea
pie	η πίτα	ee peeta
pillow	το μαξιλάρι	to makseelaree
platform	η αποβάθρα	ee apovathra
to play	παίζω	pezo
please	παρακαλώ	parakalo
pleased	ευχαριστημένος	efkhareesteemenos
police	η αστυνομία	ee asteenomeea
police station	το αστυνομικό τμήμα	to asteenomeeko tmeema
pool (for swimming)	η πισίνα	ee peeseena
pork	το χοιρινό	to kheereeno
port (harbour)	το λιμάνι	to leemanee
to post (letter)	ταχυδρομώ	takheedhromo
postcard	η καρτποστάλ	ee kartpostal
postcode	ο κωδικός	o kodheekos
post office	το ταχυδρομείο	to takheedhromeeo

pound (money)	η λίρα	ee leera
to prefer	προτιμώ	proteemo
pregnant	έγκυος	engeeos
to prepare	ετοιμάζω	eteemazo
prescription	η συνταγή	ee seendaghee
present (gift)	το δώρο	to dhoro
pretty	ωραίος	oreos
price	η τιμή	ee teemee
price list	ο τιμοκατάλογος	o teemokataloghos
private	ιδιωτικός	eedheeoteekos
problem	το πρόβλημα	to provleema
prohibited	απαγορευμένος	apaghorevmenos
to pronounce	προφέρω	profero
how do you pronounce this?	πώς το προφέρετε;	pos to proferete?
public	δημόσιος	dheemoseeos
public holiday	η γιορτή	ee yortee
purse	το πορτοφόλι	to portofolee
to push	σπρώχνω	sprokhno
to put	βάζω	vazo
to put down	βάζω κάτω	vazo kato

Q

quality	η ποιότητα	ee peeoteeta
question	η ερώτηση	ee eroteesee
queue	η ουρά	ee oora
quick	γρήγορος	ghreeghoros
quickly	γρήγορα	ghreeghora
quiet	ήσυχος	eeseekhos

R

radio	το ραδιόφωνο	to radhyofono
railway station	ο σιδηροδρομικός σταθμός	o seedheerodhro-meekos stathmos
rain	η βροχή	ee vrokhee
raining: *it's raining*	βρέχει	vrekhee
rare	σπάνιος	spanyos
(steak)	μισοψημένος	meesopseemenos
rate	ο ρυθμός	o reethmos
rate of exchange	η ισοτιμία	ee eesoteemeea
raw	ωμός	omos
razor	το ξυράφι	to kseerafee
to read	διαβάζω	dheeavazo
ready	έτοιμος	eteemos
real	πραγματικός	praghmateekos
receipt	η απόδειξη	ee apodheeksee
reception (desk)	η ρεσεψιόν	ee resepsyon
to recommend	συνιστώ	seeneesto
red	κόκκινος	kokeenos
reduction	η έκπτωση	ee ekptosee
refund	η επιστροφή χρημάτων	ee epeestrofee khreematon
registered (letter)	συστημένο	seesteemeno
relations (family)	οι συγγενείς	ee seenghenees
to relax	ξεκουράζομαι	ksekoorazome
to remember	θυμάμαι	theemame
to rent	νοικιάζω	neekyazo
to repair	επιδιορθώνω	epeedheeorthono

to repeat	επαναλαμβάνω	epanalamvano
reservation	η κράτηση	ee krateesee
to reserve	κρατώ	krato
reserved	κρατημένος	krateemenos
rest	ξεκούραση	ksekoorasee
the rest (the others)	οι υπόλοιποι	ee eepoleepee
to rest	ξεκουράζομαι	ksekoorazome
restaurant	το εστιατόριο	to esteeatoreeo
retired	συνταξιούχος	seendaksyookhos
to return (go back, give back)	επιστρέφω	epeestrefo
return ticket	το εισιτήριο με επιστροφή	to eeseeteereeo me epeestrofee
rice	το ρύζι	to reezee
rich (person, food)	πλούσιος	plooseeos
right (correct, accurate)	σωστός	sostos
(on/to the) right	δεξιά	dheksya
road	ο δρόμος	o dhromos
road map	ο οδικός χάρτης	o odheekos khartees
roast	το ψητό	to pseeto
room (in house, etc.)	το δωμάτιο	to dhomateeo
(space)	ο χώρος	o khoros
rosé	ροζέ	roze
round (shape)	στρογγυλός	strongeelos
round Greece	γύρω στην Ελλάδα	yeero steen eladha
to run	τρέχω	trekho

S

sad	λυπημένος	leepeemenos
safe *adj* (harmless)	αβλαβής	avlavees
(not dangerous)	ακίνδυνος	akeendheenos
(secure, sure)	ασφαλής	asfalees
salad	η σαλάτα	ee salata
salt	το αλάτι	to alatee
same	ίδιος	eedhyos
sand	η άμμος	ee amos
sauce	η σάλτσα	ee saltsa
to say	λέω	leo
Scotland	η Σκοτία	ee skoteea
Scottish (person)	ο Σκοτσέζος/η Σκοτσέζα	o skotsezos/ee skotseza
sculpture	το γλυπτό	to ghleepto
sea	η θάλασσα	ee thalasa
seafood	τα θαλασσινά	ta thalaseena
seaside (beach, seafront)	η παραλία	ee paraleea
seat (in theatre)	η θέση	ee thesee
(in car, etc.)	το κάθισμα	to katheesma
second	δεύτερος	dhefteros
to see	βλέπω	vlepo
to sell	πουλώ	poolo
send	στέλνω	stelno
to serve	σερβίρω	serveero
service (in restaurant, etc.)	η εξυπηρέτηση	ee ekseepeereteesee
shallow	ρηχός	reekhos

shampoo	το σαμπουάν	to sambooan
to share	μοιράζω	meerazo
shaver	η ξυριστική μηχανή	ee kseereesteekee meekhanee
she	αυτή	aftee
sheet	το σεντόνι	to sendonee
ship	το πλοίο	to pleeo
shirt	το πουκάμισο	to pookameeso
shoe	το παπούτσι	to papootsee
shop	το μαγαζί	to maghazee
to shop	ψωνίζω	psoneezo
short	κοντός	kondos
show (in theatre, etc.)	η παράσταση	ee parastasee
to show	δείχνω	dheekhno
shower (in bath)	το ντους	to doos
(rain)	η μπόρα	ee bora
shut (closed)	κλειστός	kleestos
to shut	κλείνω	kleeno
sick (ill)	άρρωστος	arostos
to be sick (vomit)	κάνω εμετό	kano emeto
sign (roadsign, notice, etc.)	η πινακίδα	ee peenakeedha
signature	η υπογραφή	ee eepoghrafee
silver	ασημένιος	aseemenyos
to sing	τραγουδώ	traghoodho
single (not married)	ελεύθερος	eleftheros
single bed	το μονό κρεβάτι	to mono krevatee
single room	το μονόκλινο δωμάτιο	to monokleeno dhomateeo

sister	η αδελφή	ee adhelfee
to sit (down)	κάθομαι	kathome
size (of clothes, shoes)	το νούμερο	to noomero
skin	το δέρμα	to dherma
skirt	η φούστα	ee foosta
sky	ο ουρανός	o ooranos
to sleep	κοιμούμαι	keemoome
slice	η φέτα	ee feta
slow	σιγά	seegha
small	μικρός	meekros
smell	η μυρωδιά	ee meerodhya
smile	το χαμόγελο	to khamoyelo
to smile	χαμογελώ	khamoyelo
smoke	ο καπνός	o kapnos
to smoke	καπνίζω	kapneezo
snow	το χιόνι	to khyonee
soap	το σαπούνι	to sapoonee
soft drink	το αναψυκτικό	to anapseekteeko
some	μερικοί	mereekee
someone	κάποιος	kapyos
something	κάτι	katee
sometimes	κάποτε	kapote
son	ο γιος	o yos
song	το τραγούδι	to traghoodhee
soon	σύντομα	seendoma
as soon as possible	το συντομότερο	to seendomotero
sooner	νωρίτερα	noreetera

sorry: *I'm sorry* (apology)	συγγνώμη	seeghnomee
soup	η σούπα	ee soopa
south	ο νότος	o notos
to speak	μιλώ	meelo
special	ειδικός	eedheekos
special needs	ειδικές ανάγκες	eedheekes anangkes
speed	η ταχύτητα	ee takheeteeta
speed limit	το όριο ταχύτητας	to oreeo takheeteetas
spirits	τα οινοπνευματώδη ποτά	ta eenopnevmatodhee pota
spoon	το κουτάλι	to kootalee
sport	το σπορ	to spor
spring (season)	η άνοιξη	ee aneeksee
square (in town)	η πλατεία	ee plateea
stamp	το γραμματόσημο	to ghramatoseemo
to start	αρχίζω	arkheezo
starter (in meal)	το ορεκτικό	to orekteeko
station	ο σταθμός	o stathmos
to stay	μένω	meno
steak	η μπριζόλα	ee breezola
sterling	η αγγλική λίρα	ee angleekee leera
still (yet)	ακόμα	akoma
(immobile)	ακίνητος	akeeneetos
(water)	μη αεριούχο	mee aereeookho
to stop	σταματώ	stamato
straight: *straight on*	ευθεία	eftheea
strawberry	η φράουλα	ee fraoola

street	ο δρόμος	o dhromos
street plan	ο οδικός χάρτης	o odheekos khartees
strong	δυνατός	dheenatos
student	ο φοιτητής/η φοιτήτρια	o feeteetees/ee feeteetreea
sugar	η ζάχαρη	ee zakharee
suitcase	η βαλίτσα	ee valeetsa
summer	το καλοκαίρι	to kalokeree
sun	ο ήλιος	o eeleeos
to sunbathe	κάνω ηλιοθε-ραπεία	kano eeleeothera-peea
sunburn (painful)	το κάψιμο από τον ήλιο	to kapseemo apo ton eeleeo
suncream	η αντιηλιακή κρέμα	ee andee-eeleeakee krema
sunglasses	τα γυαλιά του ήλιου	ta yalya too eeleeoo
sunny (weather)	ηλιόλουστος	eeleeoloostos
sunrise	η ανατολή	ee anatolee
sunset	το ηλιοβασίλεμα	to eeleeovaseelema
sunshade	η ομπρέλα	ee ombrela
supermarket	το σούπερμάρκετ	to supermarket
supper	το δείπνο	to dheepno
surfing	το σέρφινγκ	to serfeeng
surname	το επώνυμο	to eponeemo
to sweat	ιδρώνω	eedhrono
sweater	το πουλόβερ	to poolover
sweet (dessert)	το γλυκό	to ghleeko
to swim	κολυμπώ	koleembo
swimming pool	η πισίνα	ee peeseena

swimsuit	το μαγιό	to mayo
to switch on	ανάβω	anavo
to switch off	σβήνω	sveeno
swollen (ankle, etc.)	πρησμένος	preesmenos

T

table	το τραπέζι	to trapezee
tablet	το χάπι	to khapee
to take	παίρνω	perno
to take out (from bank account)	βγάζω, αποσύρω	vghazo, aposeero
to talk	μιλώ	meelo
tall	ψηλός	pseelos
to taste	δοκιμάζω	dhokeemazo
taste noun	η γεύση	ee yefsee
taxi	το ταξί	to taksee
tea	το τσάι	to tsaee
to teach	διδάσκω	dheedhasko
teacher	ο δάσκαλος/η δασκάλα	o dhaskalos/ee dhaskala
teeth	τα δόντια	ta dhondya
telephone	το τηλέφωνο	to teelefono
telephone call	το τηλεφώνημα	to teelefoneema
television	η τηλεόραση	ee teeleorasee
to tell	λέγω	legho
(story)	διηγούμαι	dhee-eeghoome
temperature	η θερμοκρασία	ee thermokraseea
to have a temperature	έχω πυρετό	ekho peereto

temporary	προσωρινός	prosoreenos
tennis	το τένις	to tenees
tent	η σκηνή	ee skeenee
to text	στέλνω μήνυμα	stelno meeneema
I'll text you	θα σου στείλω μήνυμα	tha soo steelo meeneema
thank you	ευχαριστώ	efkhareesto
that	εκείνος	ekeenos
that book	εκείνο το βιβλίο	ekeeno to veevleeo
that one	εκείνο	ekeeno
theatre	το θέατρο	to theatro
then	τότε	tote
there	εκεί	ekee
there is	υπάρχει	eeparkhee
there are	υπάρχουν	eeparkhoon
these (feminine)	αυτοί/	afta/
(masculine)	αυτές/	aftee/
(neuter)	αυτά	aftes
these books	αυτά τα βιβλία	afta ta veevleea
they	αυτοί	aftee
thief	ο κλέφτης	o kleftees
thing	το πράγμα	to praghma
thirsty: *I'm thirsty*	διψάω	dheepsao
this (masculine)	αυτός/	aftos/
(feminine)	αυτή/	aftee/
(neuter)	αυτό	afto
this book	αυτό το βιβλίο	afto to veevleeo
this one	αυτό	afto

those	εκείνοι	ekeenee
those books	εκείνα τα βιβλία	ekeena ta veevleea
through	διαμέσου	dheeamesoo
ticket	το εισιτήριο	to eeseeteereeo
tie	η γραβάτα	ee ghravata
till (cash)	το ταμείο	to tameeo
till (until)	μέχρι	mekhree
time (by the clock)	η ώρα	ee ora
what time is it?	τι ώρα είναι;	tee ora eene?
timetable (buses, trains, etc.)	το δρομολόγιο	to dromoloyeeo
(school, shop opening hours, etc.)	το ωράριο	to orareeo
tip (to waiter, etc.)	το πουρμπουάρ	to poorbooar
tired	κουρασμένος	koorasmenos
tissue	το χαρτομάντηλο	to khartomandeelo
to	σε	se
to Greece	στην Ελλάδα	steen eladha
to the (masculine)	στο/	sto/
(feminine)	στη/	stee/
(neuter)	στο	sto
tobacco	ο καπνός	o kapnos
together	μαζί	mazee
toilet	η τουαλέτα	ee tooaleta
toilet paper	το χαρτί υγείας	to khartee eeyeeas
toll	τα διόδια	ta dheeodheea
tomato	η ντομάτα	ee domata
tomorrow	αύριο	avreeo
tonight	απόψε	apopse

too (also)	επίσης	epeesees
(too much)	πάρα πολύ	para polee
tooth	το δόντι	to dhondee
toothache	ο πονόδοντος	o ponodhondos
toothbrush	η οδοντόβουρτσα	ee odhontovoortsa
toothpaste	η οδοντόκρεμα	ee odhondokrema
top	το πάνω μέρος	to pano meros
(of mountain)	η κορυφή	ee koreefee
total	το σύνολο	to seenolo
tour	η εκδρομή	ee ekdhromee
tourist	ο τουρίστας/η τουρίστρια	o tooreestas/ee tooreestreea
tourist office	το τουριστικό γραφείο	to tooreesteeko ghrafeeo
town	η πόλη	ee polee
town centre	το κέντρο της πόλης	to kendro tees polees
town plan	ο χάρτης της πόλης	o khartees tees polees
toy	το παιχνίδι	to pekhneedhee
traditional	παραδοσιακός	paradhoseeakos
traffic	η κυκλοφορία	ee keekloforeea
traffic lights	τα φανάρια (της τροχαίας)	ta fanarya (tees trokheas)
train	το τρένο	to treno
to translate	μεταφράζω	metafrazo
to travel	ταξιδεύω	takseedhevo
travel agent	ο ταξιδιωτικός πράκτορας	o takseedhyoteekos praktoras
tree	το δέντρο	to dhendro
trip	η εκδρομή	ee ekdhromee

trouble	ο μπελάς	o belas
trousers	το παντελόνι	to pandelonee
true	αληθινός	aleetheenos
to try	προσπαθώ	prospatho
to try on	δοκιμάζω	dhokeemazo
T-shirt	το μπλουζάκι	to bloozakee
to turn	στρίβω	streevo
to turn off (on a journey)	στρίβω	streevo
(radio, etc.)	κλείνω	kleeno
(engine, light)	σβήνω	sveeno
to turn on (radio, TV)	ανοίγω	aneegho
(engine, light)	ανάβω	anavo
TV	η τηλεόραση	ee teeleorasee
twice	δύο φορές	dheeo fores
twin-bedded	το δίκλινο δωμάτιο	to dheekleeno dhomateeo

U

ugly	άσχημος	askheemos
umbrella	η ομπρέλα	ee ombrela
uncle	ο θείος	o theeos
uncomfortable	άβολος	avolos
under	κάτω από	kato apo
underground (railway)	το μετρό	to metro
to understand	καταλαβαίνω	katalaveno
underwear	τα εσώρουχα	ta esorookha

unemployed	άνεργος	anerghos
United States	οι Ηνωμένες Πολιτείες	ee eenomenes poleeteeyes
university	το πανεπιστήμιο	to panepeesteemeeo
until	μέχρι/έως	mekhree/eos
upstairs	πάνω	pano
urgently	επειγόντως	epeeghondos
to use	χρησιμοποιώ	khreeseemopeeo
useful	χρήσιμος	khreeseemos
usually	συνήθως	seeneethos

V

vacancy (room)	το διαθέσιμο δωμάτιο	to dheeatheseemo dhomateeo
valuable	πολύτιμος	poleeteemos
value	η αξία	ee akseea
VAT	ο ΦΠΑ	o fee pee a
vegetables	τα λαχανικά	ta lakhaneeka
vegetarian	ο χορτοφάγος	o khortofaghos
very	πολύ	polee
video	το βίντεο	to veedeo
view	η θέα	ee thea
villa	η βίλα	ee veela
village	το χωριό	to khoryo
visa	η βίζα	ee veesa
visit	επίσκεψη	ee epeeskepsee
to visit	επισκέπτομαι	epeeskeptome
voice	η φωνή	ee fonee

to wait for	περιμένω	pereemeno
waiter	το γκαρσόνι	to garsonee
waiting room	η αίθουσα αναμονής	ee ethoosa anamonees
waitress	η σερβιτόρα	ee serveetora
Wales	η Ουαλία	ee ooaleea
walk	ο περίπατος	o pereepatos
to walk	περπατώ	perpato
wall	ο τοίχος	o teekhos
wallet	το πορτοφόλι	to portofolee
to want	θέλω	thelo
warm	ζεστός	zestos
to wash (clothes)	πλένω	pleno
(oneself)	πλένομαι	plenome
watch noun	το ρολόι	to roloee
to watch (TV)	βλέπω	vlepo
(someone's luggage)	προσέχω	prosekho
water	το νερό	to nero
watermelon	το καρπούζι	to karpoozee
way (method)	ο τρόπος	o tropos
this way	από 'δω	apodho
that way	από 'κει	apokee
we	εμείς	emees
weak	αδύνατος	adheenatos
to wear	φορώ	foro
weather	ο καιρός	o keros
wedding	ο γάμος	o ghamos

week	η εβδομάδα	ee evdhomadha
weekend	το σαββατοκύριακο	to savatokeeryako
weekly (rate, etc.)	εβδομαδιαίος	evdhomadhee-eos
weight	το βάρος	to varos
welcome	καλώς ήλθατε	kalos eelthate
well (healthy)	καλά	kala
Welsh (person)	ο Ουαλός/η Ουαλή	o ooalos/ee ooalee
west	η δύση	ee dheesee
what	τι	tee
what is it?	τι είναι;	tee eene?
wheelchair	η αναπηρική καρέκλα	ee anapeereekee karekla
when?	πότε;	pote?
where?	πού;	poo?
which? (masculine)	ποιος;	pyos?
(feminine)	ποια;	pya?
(neuter)	ποιο;	pyo?
which is it?	ποιο είναι;	pyo eene?
while	ενώ	eno
white	άσπρος	aspros
who?	ποιος;	pyos?
whole	όλος	olos
whose: whose is it?	ποιανού είναι;	pyanoo eene?
why?	γιατί;	yatee?
wide	πλατύς	platees
wife	η σύζυγος	ee seezeeghos
wind	ο αέρας	o a-eras

window	το παράθυρο	to paratheero
wine	το κρασί	to krasee
winter	ο χειμώνας	o kheemonas
with	με	me
without	χωρίς	khorees
woman	η γυναίκα	ee yeeneka
word	η λέξη	ee leksee
work	η δουλειά	ee dhoolya
to work (person)	δουλεύω	dhoolevo
(machine)	λειτουργεί	leetoorghee
worried	ανήσυχος	aneeseekhos
to write	γράφω	ghrafo
wrong	λάθος	lathos
you're wrong	κάνετε λάθος	kanete lathos

Y

year	ο χρόνος	o khronos
yellow	κίτρινος	keetreenos
yes	ναι	ne
yesterday	χτες	khtes
yet	ακόμα	akoma
not yet	όχι ακόμα	okhee akoma
yoghurt	το γιαούρτι	to yaoortee
you (singular plural)	εσύ/εσείς	esee/esees
young	νέος	neos
youth hostel	ο ξενώνας νεότητος	o ksenonas neoteetos

Z

| zero | το μηδέν | to meedhen |
| zone | η ζώνη | ee zonee |

Greek – English Dictionary

αA

άγαλμα (το)	aghalma	statue
αγάπη (η)	aghapee	love
αγαπώ	aghapo	to love
Αγγλία (η)	angleea	England
αγγλικός/ή/ό	angleekos/ee/o	English *(thing)*
Άγγλος/Αγγλίδα (ο/η)	anglos/angleedha	Englishman/-woman
άγιος/α/ο	agheeos/a/o	holy, saint
Άγιον Όρος (το)	agheeon oros	Mount Athos
αγορά (η)	aghora	market
αγοράζω	aghorazo	to buy
αγόρι (το)	aghoree	young boy
άδεια (η)	adheea	permit, licence
άδεια οδήγησης	adheea odheegheesees	driving licence
άδειος/α/ο	adheeos/a/o	empty
αδελφή (η)	adhelfee	sister
αδελφός (ο)	adhelfos	brother
αδίκημα (το)	adheekeema	offence
αέρας (ο)	aeras	wind
αεροδρόμιο (το)	aerodhromeeo	airport
αεροπλάνο (το)	aeroplano	aeroplane
αεροπορικό εισιτήριο (το)	aeroporeeko eeseeteereeo	air ticket
Αθήνα (η)	atheena	Athens
αθλητικό κέντρο (το)	athleeteeko kendro	sports centre

αθλητισμός (ο)	athleeteesmos	sports
Αιγαίο (το)	egheo	the Aegean Sea
αίμα (το)	ema	blood
αίτηση (η)	eteesee	application
ακούω	akoo-o	to hear
Ακρόπολη (η)	akropolee	the Acropolis
ακτή (η)	aktee	beach, shore
αλάτι (το)	alatee	salt
αλλαγή (η)	alaghee	change
αλλάζω	alazo	to change
αμάξι (το)	amaksee	car, vehicle
αμερικάνικος/η/ο	amereekaneekos/ee/o	American *(thing)*
Αμερικανός/ Αμερικανίδα	amereekanos/ amereekaneedha	American *(man/ woman)*
Αμερική (η)	amereekee	America
αμέσως	amesos	at once, immediately
άμμος (η)	amos	sand
αν	an	if
ανάβω	anavo	to switch on
αίθουσα αναμονής	ethoosa anamonees	waiting room
ανάπηρος/η/ο	anapeeros/ee/o	handicapped, disabled
ανατολή (η)	anatolee	east, sunrise
ανατολικός/ή/ό	anatoleekos/ee/o	eastern
αναψυκτικό (το)	anapseekteeko	soft drink
άνδρας (ο)	andhras	man, male
ανθοπωλείο (το)	anthopoleeo	florist's

άνθρωπος (ο)	anthropos	person
ανοίγω	aneegho	to open
άνοιξη (η)	aneeksee	spring *(season)*
ανταλλαγή (η)	andalaghee	exchange
αντιβιοτικά (τα)	andeeveeoteeka	antibiotics
αντίγραφο (το)	andeeghrafo	copy
αντίκες (οι)	anteekes	antiques
αντίο	andeeo	goodbye
απαγορεύω	apaghorevo	to forbid: no...
απάντηση (η)	apanteesee	answer
απέναντι	apenandee	opposite
απογείωση (η)	apogheeoose	takeoff
απόγευμα (το)	apoyevma	afternoon
απόδειξη (η)	apodheeksee	receipt
αποσκευές (οι)	aposkeves	luggage
αναζήτηση αποσκευών	anazeeteesee aposkevon	left-luggage *(office)*
απόψε	apopse	tonight
αργότερα	arghotera	later
αρέσω	areso	to please
μου αρέσει	moo aresee	I like
δεν μου αρέσει	dhen moo aresee	I don't like
σου αρέσει	soo aresee	you like
δεν σου αρέσει	dhen soo aresee	you don't like
αριθμός (ο)	areethmos	number
αριθμός τηλεφώνου	areethmos teelefonoo	telephone number
αριστερά	areestera	left *(opposite of right)*

αρνί (το)	arnee	lamb
αρρώστια (η)	arosteea	illness
άρρωστος/η/ο	arostos/ee/o	ill
αρχαίος/α/ο	arkheos/a/o	ancient
αρχή (η)	arkhee	start, beginning
αρχίζω	arkheezo	to begin, to start
άρωμα (το)	aroma	perfume
ασανσέρ (το)	asanser	lift, elevator
ασθενής (ο/η)	asthenees	patient
ασπιρίνη (η)	aspeereenee	aspirin
άσπρος/η/ο	aspros/ee/o	white
αστυνομία (η)	asteenomeea	police
αστυνομία αλλοδαπών	asteenomeea alodhapon	immigration police
Ελληνική αστυνομία	eleeneekee asteenomeea	Greek police
αστυνομικό τμήμα (το)	asteenomeeko tmeema	police station
αστυνόμος (ο)	asteenomos	policeman
ασφάλεια (η)	asfaleea	insurance, fuse
ιατρική ασφάλιση	eeatreekee asfaleesee	medical insurance
άτομο (το)	atomo	person
ατύχημα (το)	ateekheema	accident
αυτοκίνητο (το)	aftokeeneeto	car
ενοικιάσεις αυτοκινήτων	eneekyasees aftokeeneeton	car hire
συνεργείο αυτοκινήτων	seenergheeon aftokeeneeton	car repairs

αυτοκινητό- δρομος (ο)	aftokeeneeto- dhromos	motorway
αυτόματος/η/ο	aftomatos/ee/o	automatic
άφιξη (η)	afeeksee	arrival

ßB

βαγόνι το	vaghonee	carriage *(train)*
βάζω	vazo	to put
βαλίτσα (η)	valeetsa	suitcase
βαρέλι: μπύρα από βαρέλι	beera apo varelee	draught beer
βαρελίσιο κρασί (το)	vareleeseeo krasee	house wine
βάρκα (η)	varka	boat
βάρος (το)	varos	weight
βγάζω	vghazo	to take off
βγαίνω	vgheno	to go out
βενζίνη (η)	venzeenee	petrol, gasoline
βήχας (ο)	veekhas	cough
βιβλίο (το)	veevleeo	book
βιβλιοπωλείο (το)	veevleeopoleeo	bookshop
βλέπω	vlepo	to see
βοήθεια (η)	voeetheea	help
οδική βοήθεια	odheekee voeetheea	breakdown service
πρώτες βοήθειες	protes voeethee-es	casualty *(hospital)*
βόλτα (η)	volta	walk, drive, trip
βόρειος/α/ο	voreeos/a/o	northern
βορράς (ο)	voras	north

βουνό (το)	voono	mountain
βράδυ (το)	vradhee	evening
βραδινό (το)	vradheeno	evening meal
βράζω	vrazo	to boil
Βρετανία (η)	vretaneea	Britain
Βρετανός/ Βρετανίδα (ο/η)	vretanos/ vretaneedha	British (man/woman)
βρίσκω	vreesko	to find
βρόμικος/η/ο	vromeekos/ee/o	dirty
βροχή (η)	vrokhee	rain

γΓ

γάλα (το)	ghala	milk
γαλάζιος/α/ο	ghalazeeos/a/o	blue, light blue
γάμος (ο)	ghamos	wedding, marriage
γεια σας	ya sas	hello, goodbye (formal)
γεια σου	ya soo	hello, goodbye (informal)
γεμάτος/η/ο	yematos/ee/o	full
γενέθλια (τα)	yenethleea	birthday
γενικός/ή/ό	yeneekos/ee/o	general
γέννηση (η)	yeneesee	birth
γεύμα (το)	yevma	meal
γέφυρα (η)	yefeera	bridge
για	ya	for
γιαγιά (η)	yaya	grandmother
γιατί;	yatee?	why?

γιατρός (ο/η)	yatros	doctor
γιορτή (η)	yortee	festival, celebration, name day
γιος (ο)	yos	son
γκάζι (το)	gazee	accelerator *(car)*, gas
γκαλερί	galeree	art gallery, art sales
γκαράζ (το)	garaz	garage
γκαρσόν (το)/ γκαρσόνι (το)	garson/garsonee	waiter
γλυκός/ιά/ό	ghleekos/ya/o	sweet
γλυκό (το)/γλυκά (τα)	ghleeko/ghleeka	cakes and pastries, desserts
γλυπτική (η)	ghleepteekee	sculpture
γλώσσα (η)	ghlosa	tongue, language, sole *(fish)*
γονείς (οι)	ghonees	parents
γράμμα (το)	ghrama	letter
γράμμα κατεπείγον	ghrama katepeeghon	express letter
γράμμα συστημένο	ghrama seesteemeno	recorded delivery
γραμμάριο (το)	ghramareeo	gram
γραμματοκι- βώτιο (το)	ghramatokeevoteeo	letter box
γραμματόσημο (το)	ghramatoseemo	stamp
γραφείο (το)	ghrafeeo	office, desk
Γραφείο Τουρισμού	ghrafeeo tooreesmoo	Tourist Office
γράφω	ghrafo	to write

γρήγορα	ghreegora	quickly
γρίπη (η)	ghreepee	influenza
γυαλί (το)	yalee	glass
γυαλιά (τα)	yalya	glasses
γυαλιά ηλίου	yalya eeleeoo	sunglasses
γυμναστήριο (το)	yeemnasteereeo	gym
γυναίκα (η)	yeeneka	woman
γύρω	yeero	round, about
γωνία (η)	ghoneea	corner

δΔ

δάσος (το)	dhasos	forest, wood
δείπνο (το)	dheepno	dinner
δέκα	dheka	ten
Δελφοί (οι)	dhelfee	Delphi
δεν	dhen	not
δεξιά	dhekseea	right *(opposite of left)*
δέρμα (το)	dherma	skin, leather
δεσποινίς/ δεσποινίδα (η)	dhespeenees/ dhespeeneedha	Miss
δεύτερος/η/ο	dhefteros/ee/o	second
δήλωση (η)	dheelosee	announcement
είδη προς δήλωση	eedhee pros dheelosee	goods to declare
ουδέν προς δήλωση	oodhen pros dheelosee	nothing to declare
δημαρχείο (το)	dheemarkheeo	town hall
δημόσιος/α/ο	dheemoseeos	public/state

217

δημόσια έργα	dheemoseea ergha	road works
δημόσιος κήπος	dheemoseeos keepos	public gardens
δημοτικός/ή/ό	dheemoteekos	public/municipal
Δημοτική Αγορά	dheemoteekee aghora	public market
διάβαση (η)	dheeavasee	crossing
διαβατήριο (το)	dheeavateereeo	passport
διαβήτης (ο)	dheeaveetees	diabetes
διαδρομή (η)	dheeadhromee	route
διακεκριμένη θέση	dheeakekreemenee thesee	business class
διακοπές (οι)	dheeakopes	holidays
διάλειμμα (το)	dheealeema	interval, break
διαμέρισμα (το)	dheeamereesma	flat, apartment
διανυχτερεύει	dheeaneekhterevee	open all night
διασκέδαση (η)	dheeaskedhasee	entertainment
κέντρο δια-σκεδάσεως	kendro dheeaskedaseos	nightclub
διασταύρωση (η)	dheeastavrosee	crossroads, junction
διεθνής/ής/ές	dhee-ethnees/ees/es	international
διεύθυνση (η)	dhee-eftheensee	address
διευθυντής (ο)	dhee-eftheentees	manager
δικαστήριο (το)	dheekasteereeo	court
δικηγόρος (ο/η)	dheekeeghoros	lawyer
δίνω	dheeno	to give
δίπλα	dheepla	next to
διπλός/ή/ό	dheeplos/ee/o	double
διπλό δωμάτιο	dheeplo domateeo	double room

διπλό κρεβάτι	dheeplo krevatee	double bed
δολάριο (το)	dholareeo	dollar
δόντι (το)	dhondee	tooth
δρομολόγιο (το)	dhromologheeo	timetable, route
δρόμος (ο)	dhromos	street, way
δύση (η)	dheesee	west, sunset
δύσκολος/η/ο	dheeskolos/ee/o	difficult
δυστύχημα (το)	dheesteekheema	accident, mishap
δυτικός/ή/ό	dheeteekos/ee/o	western
Δωδεκάνησα (τα)	dhodhekaneesa	the Dodecanese
δωμάτιο (το)	dhomateeo	room
δωρεάν	dhorean	free of charge
δώρο (το)	dhoro	present, gift

εΕ

εβδομάδα (η)	evdhomadha	week
εγγύηση (η)	engheeyeesee	guarantee
εδώ	edho	here
εθνικός/ή/ό	ethneekos/ee/o	national
Εθνικό Θέατρο	ethneeko theatro	National Theatre
εθνική οδός	ethneekee odhos	motorway
έθνος (το)	ethnos	nation
εθνικότητα	ethneekoteeta	nationality
ειδικός/ή/ό	eedheekos/ee/o	special, specialist
είδος (το)	eedhos	kind, sort
είδη	eedhee	goods
είμαι	eeme	to be

εισιτήριο (το)	eeseeteereeo	ticket
εκδόσεις εισιτηρίων	ekdhosees eeseeteereeon	ticket office
εκεί	ekee	there
έκθεση (η)	ekthesee	exhibition
εκκλησία (η)	ekleeseea	church, chapel
έκπτωση (η)	ekptosee	discount
εκτελούνται έργα	ekteloonde ergha	road works
εκτός	ektos	except, unless
εκτός λειτουργίας	ektos leetoorgheeas	out of order
έλα!	ela!	come on! *(singular)*
ελάτε!	elate!	come on! *(plural)*
ελαιόλαδο (το)	eleoladho	olive oil
ελαττώνω	elatono	to reduce, to decrease
ελαττώσατε ταχύτητα	elatosate takheeteeta	reduce speed
έλεγχος (ο)	elengkhos	control
έλεγχος διαβατηρίων	elengkhos dheeavateereeon	passport control
έλεγχος εισιτηρίων	elengkhos eeseeteereeon	check-in
ελεύθερος/η/ο	eleftheros/ee/o	single, free
ελιά (η)	elya	olive, olive tree
Ελλάδα (η)	eladha	Greece
Έλληνας/ Ελληνίδα (ο/η)	eleenas/eleeneedha	Greek *(man/woman)*
ελληνικά (τα)	eleeneeka	Greek *(language)*
ελληνικός/ή/ό	eleeneekos/ee/o	Greek *(thing)*

μπρός	embros	forward, in front, 'hello!' *(on phone)*
νας/μία/ένα	enas/meea/ena	one
νήλικος (ο)	eneeleekos	adult
ννέα/εννιά	enea/enya	nine
νοικιάζω	eneekeeazo	to rent, to hire
νοικιάζεται	eneekeeazete	to let
νοικιάσεις	eneekeeasees	for hire
νοίκιο (το)	eneekeeo	rent
ντάξει	endaksee	all right, OK
ντυπο (το)	endeepo	form *(to fill in)*
ξι	eksee	six
ξυπηρέτηση (η)	ekseepeereteesee	service
ξω	ekso	out, outside
ξωτερικός: το εξωτερικό	to eksotereeko	abroad
OT	eot	Greek Tourist Organisation
πάγγελμα (το)	epanghelma	occupation, profession
πείγον/ επείγουσα	epeeghon/ epeeghoosa	urgent, express
πείγοντα περιστατικά	epeeghonta pereestateeka	casualty department
πιβάτης/τρια (ο/η)	epeevatees/treea	passenger
πιβεβαιώνω	epeeveveono	to confirm
πιβίβαση (η)	epeeveevasee	boarding
άρτα επιβιβάσεως	karta epeeveevaseos	boarding card

επειδή	epeedhee	because
επιδόρπιο (το)	epeedhorpeeo	dessert
επικίνδυνος/η/ο	epeekeendeenos/ee/o	dangerous
επίσης	epeesees	also, the same to yo
επισκέπτης (ο)	epeeskeptees	visitor
επίσκεψη (η)	epeeskepsee	visit
επιστροφή (η)	epeestrofee	return, return ticket
επιστροφές	epeestrofes	returned goods, refunds
επιταγή (η)	epeetaghee	cheque, invoice
επόμενος/η/ο	epomenos/ee/o	next
εποχή (η)	epokhee	season
επτά/εφτά	epta/efta	seven
Επτάνησα (τα)	eptaneesa	Ionian Islands
επώνυμο (το)	eponeemo	surname, last name
έργα (τα)	ergha	works
έργο	ergho	film, play, TV program
εργοστάσιο (το)	erghostaseeo	factory
έρχομαι	erkhome	to come
ερώτηση (η)	eroteesee	question
εστιατόριο (το)	esteeatoreeo	restaurant
εσώρουχα (τα)	esorookha	underwear, lingerie
εσωτερικός: πτήσεις εσωτερικού	pteesees esotereekoo	domestic flights
έτος (το)	etos	year
έτσι	etsee	so, like this

ευθεία (η)	eftheea	straight
ευθύνη (η)	eftheenee	responsibility
ευκαιρία (η)	efkereea	opportunity, bargain
εύκολος/η/ο	efkolos/ee/o	easy
Ευρωπαϊκή Ένωση	evropaeekee enosee	European Union
ευρωπαϊκός/ή/ό	evropaeekos/ee/o	European
Ευρώπη (η)	evropee	Europe
ευχαριστώ	efkhareesto	thank you
εφημερίδα (η)	efeemereedha	newspaper
έχω	ekho	to have

ζΖ

ζάλη (η)	zalee	dizziness
ζαμπόν (το)	zambon	ham
ζάχαρη (η)	zakharee	sugar
ζαχαροπλαστείο (το)	zakharoplasteeo	patisserie
ζέστη (η)	zestee	heat
κάνει ζέστη	kanee zestee	it's hot
ζευγάρι (το)	zevgharee	couple
ζημιά (η)	zeemya	damage
ζητώ	zeeto	to ask, to seek
ζυμαρικά (τα)	zeemareekha	pasta products
ζωγραφιά (η)	zoghrafya	picture, painting
ζώνη (η)	zonee	belt
ζώνη ασφαλείας	zonee asfaleeas	safety belt, seat belt
ζώο (το)	zo-o	animal

223

ηΗ

η	ee	the *(with feminine nouns)*
ή	ee	or
ηλεκτρικός/ή/ό	eelektreekos/ee/o	electrical
ηλεκτρισμός (ο)	eelektreesmos	electricity
ηλεκτρονικός/ή/ό	eelektroneekos/ ee/o	electronic
ηλίαση (η)	eeleeasee	sunstroke
ηλικία (η)	eeleekeea	age
ηλιοβασίλεμα (το)	eeleeovaseelema	sunset
ηλιοθεραπεία (η)	eeleeotherapeea	sunbathing
ήλιος (ο)	eeleeos	sun
ημέρα (η)	eemera	day
ημερήσιος/α/ο	eemereeseeos/a/o	daily
ημερομηνία λήξης	eemeromeeneea leeksees	expiry date
ημιδιατροφή (η)	eemeedheeatrofee	half board
Ηνωμένο Βασίλειο (το)	eenomeno vaseeleeo	United Kingdom *(UK)*
Ηνωμένες Πολιτείες της Αμερικής	eenomenes poleetee-es tees amereekees	United States of America
ΗΠΑ		USA
ησυχία (η)	eesekheea	calm, quiet

θΘ

θάλασσα (η)	thalasa	sea
θαλάσσιο σκι	thalaseeo skee	water-skiing
θέατρο (το)	theatro	theatre

Θέλω	thelo	to want
Θεός/θεά (ο/η)	theos/thea	god/goddess
Θεραπεία (η)	therapeea	treatment
Θέρμανση (η)	thermansee	heating
Θέση (η)	thesee	place, seat
κράτηση θέσης	krateesee thesees	seat reservation
οικονομική θέση	eekonomeekee thesee	economy class
πρώτη θέση	protee thesee	first class
Θεσσαλονίκη (η)	thesaloneekee	Salonica/Thessaloniki
Θύρα (η)	theera	gate *(airport)*
Θυρίδα (η)	theereedha	ticket window

ι

ιατρική περίθαλψη (η)	eeatreekee pereethalpsee	medical treatment
ιατρός (ο/η)	yatros	doctor
ιδιοκτήτης/τρια (ο/η)	eedheeokteetees/treea	owner
ίντερνετ (το)	eenternet	internet
Ιόνιο Πέλαγος (το)	eeoneeo pelaghos	Ionian sea
ιπτάμενο δελφίνι	eeptameno dhelfeenee	hydrofoil *(flying dolphin)*
Ισθμός της Κορίνθου	eesthmos tees koreenthoo	Corinth Canal
ισοτιμία (η)	eesoteemeea	exchange rate
ιστιοπλοΐα (η)	eesteeoploeea	sailing
ιχθυοπωλείο (το)	eekhtheeopoleeo	fishmonger's

κK

κάβα (η)	kava	wine merchant, off-licence
καζίνο (το)	kazeeno	casino
καθαριστήριο (το)	kathareesteereeo	dry-cleaner's
καθαρός/ή/ό	katharos/ee/o	clean
κάθε	kathe	every, each
κάθε μέρα	kathe mera	every day
καθημερινός/ή/ό	katheemereenos/ee/o	daily
κάθισμα (το)	katheesma	seat
καθυστέρηση (η)	katheestereesee	delay
και	ke	and
καιρός (ο)	keros	weather, time
κακός/ή/ό	kakos/ee/o	bad
καλά	kala	well, all right
καλημέρα	kaleemera	good morning
καληνύχτα	kaleeneekhta	good night
καλησπέρα	kaleespera	good evening
καλοκαίρι (το)	kalokeree	summer
καλοριφέρ (το)	kaloreefer	central heating, radiator
καλοψημένο	kalopseemeno	well done *(meat)*
καμπίνα (η)	kambeena	cabin
κανάλι (το)	kanalee	canal, channel *(TV)*
κανένας	kanenas	no-one
καντίνα (η)	kanteena	mobile roadside café
κάνω	kano	to do

καπέλο (το)	kapelo	hat
καπνίζω	kapneezo	to smoke
καράβι (το)	karavee	boat, ship
κάρβουνο (το)	karvoono	coal, charcoal
στα κάρβουνα	sta karvoona	charcoal-grilled
καρδιά (η)	kardheea	heart
καρναβάλι (το)	karnavalee	carnival
καροτσάκι (το)	karotsakee	pushchair
καροτσάκι αναπηρικό	karotsakee anapeereeko	wheelchair
κάρτα (η)	karta	card, postcard
κάρτα επιβιβάσεως	karta epeeveevaseos	boarding card
πιστωτική κάρτα	peestoteekee karta	credit card
καρτοτηλέφωνο (το)	kartoteelefono	card phone
καρτποστάλ (το)	kartpostal	postcard
κάστρο (το)	kastro	castle, fortress
καταιγίδα (η)	kategheedha	storm
καταλαβαίνω	katalaveno	to understand
καταλαβαίνεις; (familiar form)	katalavenees?	do you understand?
καταλαβαίνετε; (polite form)	katalavenete?	do you understand?
κατάλογος (ο)	kataloghos	list, menu, directory
κατασκήνωση (η)	kataskeenosee	camping
κατάστημα (το)	katasteema	shop
κατεπείγον/ κατεπείγουσα	katepeeghon/ katepeeghoosa	urgent, express

κατηγορία (η)	kateghoreea	class *(of hotel)*
κατσίκα (η)	katseeka	goat
κάτω	kato	under, lower, down
καύσιμα (τα)	kafseema	fuel
καφέ	kafe	brown
καφενείο (το)	kafeneeo	coffee house
καφές (ο)	kafes	coffee *(usually Greek)*
καφές γλυκός	kafes ghleekos	sweet coffee
καφές μέτριος	kafes metreeos	medium sweet coffee
καφές σκέτος	kafes sketos	strong black coffee
καφές φραπέ	kafes frape	iced coffee (Nescafé®)
καφετέρια (η)	kafetereea	cafeteria
κεντρικός/ή/ό	kendreekos/ee/o	central
κέντρο (το)	kendro	centre
κέντρο δια-σκεδάσεως	kendro dheea-skedhaseos	nightclub
κέντρο υγείας	kendro eegheeas	health centre
αθλητικό κέντρο	athleeteeko kendro	sports centre
Κέρκυρα (η)	kerkeera	Corfu
κέρμα (το)	kerma	coin
κερνώ	kerno	to buy a drink
να κεράσω;	na keraso?	can I buy (you) a drink?
κεφάλι (το)	kefalee	head
κεφτέδες (οι)	keftedhes	meatballs
κήπος (ο)	keepos	garden
κιβώτιο (το)	keevoteeo	large box

κιλό (το)	keelo	kilo
κίνδυνος (ο)	keendheenos	danger
κινητό (το)	keeneeto	mobile phone
κίτρινος/η/ο	keetreenos/ee/o	yellow
κλείνω	kleeno	to close
κλέφτης (ο)	kleftees	thief
κλινική (η)	kleeneekee	clinic, hospital, ward
κοιμάμαι	keemame	to sleep
κόκκινος/η/ο	kokeenos/ee/o	red
κολοκυθάκι (το)	kolokeethakee	courgette, zucchini
κολύμπι (το)	koleembee	swimming
κολυμπώ	koleembo	to swim
κομμωτήριο (το)	komoteereeo	hairdresser's
κομπιούτερ (το)	kompyooter	computer
κοντά	konda	near
κόρη (η)	koree	daughter
κορίτσι (το)	koreetsee	young girl
κοσμήματα (τα)	kosmeemata	jewellery
κοστούμι (το)	kostoomee	man's suit
κότα (η)	kota	hen
κουβέρ (το)	koover	cover-charge
κουβέρτα (η)	kooverta	blanket, cover
κουζίνα (η)	koozeena	kitchen, cuisine
ελληνική κουζίνα	eleeneekee koozeena	Greek cuisine
κουνούπι (το)	koonoopee	mosquito
κουρείο (το)	kooreeo	barber's shop
κουτάλι (το)	kootalee	spoon

κουτί (το)	kootee	box
κρασί (το)	krasee	wine
κράτηση (η)	krateesee	reservation
κράτηση θέσης	krateesee thesees	seat reservation
κρέας (το)	kreas	meat
κρέας αρνίσιο	kreas arneesyo	lamb
κρέας μοσχαρίσιο	kreas moskhareesyo	beef
κρέας χοιρινό	kreas kheereeno	pork
κρεβάτι (το)	krevatee	bed
κρεβατοκάμαρα (η)	krevatokamara	bedroom
κρέμα (η)	krema	cream
κρεμμύδι (το)	kremeedhee	onion
κρεοπωλείο (το)	kreopoleeo	butcher's shop
Κρήτη (η)	kreetee	Crete
κρουαζιέρα (η)	krooazyera	cruise
κρύος/α/ο	kreeos/a/o	cold
κυβέρνηση (η)	keeverneesee	government
Κυκλάδες (οι)	keekladhes	Cyclades (islands)
κύκλος (ο)	keeklos	circle
κυκλοφορία (η)	keekloforeea	traffic, circulation
κυλικείο (το)	keeleekeeo	canteen, cafeteria
Κύπρος (η)	keepros	Cyprus
Κύπριος/Κυπρία (ο/η)	keepreeos/keepreea	from Cyprus, Cypriot (man/woman)
κυρία (η)	keereea	Mrs, lady
κύριος (ο)	keereeos	Mr, gentleman

| κωδικός (ο) | kodheekos | code |
| κωμωδία (η) | komodheea | comedy |

λΛ

λάδι (το)	ladhee	oil
λάδι ελιάς	ladhee elyas	olive oil
λαϊκός/ή/ό	laeekos/ee/o	popular, folk
λαϊκή αγορά	laeekee aghora	market
λαϊκή τέχνη	laeekee tekhnee	folk art
λαχανικά (τα)	lakhaneeka	vegetables
λεμονάδα (η)	lemonadha	lemonade
λεμόνι (το)	lemonee	lemon
λεξικό (το)	lekseeko	dictionary
λεπτό (το)	lepto	minute
λεπτός/ή/ό	leptos/ee/o	thin, slim
λευκός/ή/ό	lefkos/ee/o	white
λεφτά (τα)	lefta	money
λέω	leo	to say
λεωφορείο (το)	leoforeeo	bus
λήξη (η)	leeksee	expiry
λίγος/η/ο	leeghos/ee/o	a few, a little
λιμάνι (το)	leemanee	port, harbour
Λιμενικό Σώμα (το)	leemeneeko soma	coastguard, Port Police
λίμνη (η)	leemnee	lake
λίρα (η)	leera	pound
λίτρο (το)	leetro	litre

λογαριασμός (ο)	logharyasmos	bill
λουκάνικο (το)	lookaneeko	sausage
λουλούδι (το)	looloodhee	flower

μM

μαγαζί (το)	maghazee	shop
μαγειρεύω	magheerevo	to cook
μαγιό (το)	mayo	swimsuit
μακαρόνια (τα)	makaronya	spaghetti, pasta
μάλιστα	maleesta	yes, of course
μαλλί (το)	malee	wool
μαλλιά (τα)	malya	hair
μάλλινος/η/ο	maleenos/ee/o	woollen
μαμά (η)	mama	mum
μαντήλι (το)	mandeelee	handkerchief
μαξιλάρι (το)	makseelaree	pillow, cushion
μαργαρίνη (η)	marghareenee	margarine
μάρμαρο (το)	marmaro	marble
μαρμελάδα (η)	marmeladha	jam
μαρούλι (το)	maroolee	lettuce
μαύρος/η/ο	mavros/ee/o	black
μαχαίρι (το)	makheree	knife
μαχαιροπήρουνα (τα)	makheropeeroona	cutlery
με	me	with
μεγάλος/η/ο	meghalos	large, big
μέγαρο (το)	megharo	hall, palace, apartment block

μέγαρο μουσικής	megharo mooseekees	concert hall
μέγεθος (το)	meghethos	size
μέλι (το)	melee	honey
μενού (το)	menoo	menu
μέρα (η)	mera	day
μερίδα (η)	mereedha	portion
μέσα	mesa	in, inside
μεσάνυχτα (τα)	mesaneekhta	midnight
μεσημέρι (το)	meseemeree	midday
μεσημεριανό (το)	meseemeryano	midday meal
Μεσόγειος (η)	mesoyeeos	Mediterranean Sea
μετά	meta	after
μεταξύ	metaksee	between, among
μεταφράζω	metafrazo	to translate
μετεωρολογικό δελτίο (το)	meteorologheeko dhelteeo	weather forecast
μετρητά (τα)	metreeta	cash
μετρό (το)	metro	underground *(railway/metro)*
μηδέν	meedhen	zero
μήλο (το)	meelo	apple
μήνας (ο)	meenas	month
μήνας του μέλιτος	meenas too meleetos	honeymoon
μητέρα (η)	meetera	mother
μηχανάκι (το)	meekhanakee	moped, motorbike
μικρός/ή/ό	meekros/ee/o	small
μιλάω/μιλώ	meelao/meelo	to speak
μολύβι (το)	moleevee	pencil

233

μόλυνση (η)	moleensee	infection, pollution
μοναστήρι (το)	monasteeree	monastery
μονόδρομος (ο)	monodhromos	one-way street
μονοπάτι (το)	monopatee	path
μόνος/η/ο	monos/ee/o	alone, only
μόνο είσοδος/ έξοδος	mono eesodhos/ eksodhos	entrance/exit only
μοτοσυκλέτα (η)	motoseekleta	motorcycle
μουσείο (το)	mooseeo	museum
μουσική (η)	mooseekee	music
μπακάλης (ο)	bakalees	grocer
μπαμπάς (ο)	babas	dad
μπάνιο (το)	banyo	bathroom, bath
μπαταρία (η)	batareea	battery
μπιζέλια (τα)	beezelya	peas
μπισκότο (το)	beeskoto	biscuit
μπλε	ble	blue
μπλούζα (η)	blooza	jumper
μπουκάλι (το)	bookalee	bottle
μπριζόλα (η)	breezola	chop, steak
μπύρα (η)	beera	beer
Μυκήνες	meekeenes	Mycenae
μύτη (η)	meetee	nose
μωρό (το)	moro	baby

νΝ

ναι	ne	yes
ναός (ο)	naos	temple, church
ναυτία (η)	nafteea	travel sickness
νεκροταφείο (το)	nekrotafeeo	cemetery
νεοελληνικά (τα)	neoeleeneeka	Modern Greek
νερό (το)	nero	water
νες, νεσκαφέ (το)	nes, neskafe	instant coffee
νεφρό (το)	nefro	kidney
νησί (το)	neesee	island
νοίκι (το)	neekee	rent
νομίζω	nomeezo	to think
νόμισμα (το)	nomeesma	coin, currency
νοσοκομείο (το)	nosokomeeo	hospital
νοσοκόμος/α (ο/η)	nosokomos/a	nurse
νότος (ο)	notos	south
νούμερο (το)	noomero	number
ντους (το)	doos	shower
νυκτερινός/ή/ό	neektereenos/ee/o	all-night *(chemists, etc.)*
νύχτα (η)	neekhta	night

ξΞ

ξεκουράζω	ksekoorazo	to have a rest, to relax
ξεναγός (ο/η)	ksenaghos	guide
ξενοδοχείο (το)	ksenodhokheeo	hotel

ξένος/η/ο	ksenos/ee/o	foreign
ξέρω	ksero	to know
ξεχνώ	ksekhno	to forget
ξηρός/ή/ό	kseeros/ee/o	dry
ξύλο (το)	kseelo	wood

οΟ

οδηγός (ο)	odheeghos	driver, guidebook
οδηγώ	odheegho	to drive
οδική βοήθεια (η)	odheekee voeetheea	breakdown service
οδοντιατρείο (το)	odhondeeatreeo	dental surgery
οδοντίατρος (ο/η)	odhondeeatros	dentist
οδοντόβουρτσα (η)	odhondovoortsa	toothbrush
οδοντόκρεμα (η)	odhondokrema	toothpaste
οδός (η)	odhos	road, street
οικογένεια (η)	eekoyeneea	family
οινοπνευματώδη ποτά (τα)	eenopnevmatodhee pota	spirits
οκτώ/οχτώ	okto/okhto	eight
Ολυμπία (η)	oleempeea	Olympia
ολυμπιακός/ή/ό	oleempeeakos/ee/o	Olympic
Όλυμπος (ο)	oleempos	Mount Olympus
όμιλος (ο)	omeelos	club
ναυτικός όμιλος	nafteekos omeelos	sailing club
ομπρέλα (η)	ombrela	umbrella
όνομα (το)	onoma	name

ονοματεπώνυμο (το)	onomateponeemo	full name
οργανωμένος/η/ο	orghanomenos/ee/o	organised
όρεξη: *καλή όρεξη*	kalee oreksee	enjoy your meal!
ορθόδοξος/η/ο	orthodhoksos/ee/o	orthodox
όροι ενοικιάσεως	oree eneekeeaseos	conditions of hire
ΟΣΕ	ose	Greek Railways
ΟΤΕ	ote	Greek Telecom
ούζο (το)	oozo	ouzo
όχι	okhee	no

πΠ

παϊδάκι (το)	paeedhakee	lamb chop
πάγος (ο)	paghos	ice
παίρνω	perno	to take
παγωμένος/η/ο	paghomenos/ee/o	frozen
παγωτό (το)	paghoto	ice cream
παιδικός/ή/ό	pedheekos/ee/o	for children
παιδικά	pedheeka	children's wear
παιδικός σταθμός	pedheekos stathmos	crèche
πακέτο (το)	paketo	parcel, packet
Παναγία (η)	panagheea	the Virgin Mary
πανεπιστήμιο (το)	panepeesteemeeo	university
πανηγύρι (το)	paneeyeeree	festival
πάντα/πάντοτε	panda/pandote	always
παντελόνι (το)	pandelonee	trousers
παντοπωλείο (το)	pandopoleeo	grocer's

237

παντρεμένος/η/ο	pantremenos/ee/o	married
πάνω	pano	up, on, above
παπάς (ο)	papas	priest
πάπλωμα (το)	paploma	duvet
παππούς (ο)	papoos	grandfather
παπούτσι (το)	papootsee	shoe
παραγγέλνω	paranghelno	to order
παραγωγή: *Ελληνικής παραγωγής*	eleeneekees paraghoghees	produce of Greece
παράθυρο (το)	paratheero	window
παρακαλώ	parakalo	please
παραλία (η)	paraleea	seashore, beach
παράσταση (η)	parastasee	performance
παρέα (η)	parea	company, group
Παρθενώνας (ο)	parthenonas	the Parthenon
πάρκο (το)	parko	park
Πάσχα (το)	paskha	Easter
πατάτα (η)	patata	potato
πατέρας (ο)	pateras	father
παυσίπονο (το)	pafseepono	painkiller
πάω	pao	to go
πεζοδρόμιο (το)	pezodhromeeo	pavement
πεθαμένος/η/ο	pethamenos/ee/o	dead
Πειραιάς (ο)	peereas	Piraeus
πελάτης/ πελάτισσα (ο/η)	pelatees/pelateesa	customer
Πελοπόννησος (η)	peloponeesos	Peloponnese

περιοδικό (το)	pereeodheeko	magazine
περιοχή (η)	pereeokhee	area
περίπατος (ο)	pereepatos	walk
περίπτερο (το)	pereeptero	kiosk
πετρέλαιο (το)	petreleo	diesel fuel
πετσέτα (η)	petseta	towel
πηγαίνω	peegheno	to go
πιάτο (το)	pyato	plate, dish
πίεση αίματος	peeyesee ematos	blood pressure
πινακοθήκη (η)	peenakotheekee	art gallery
πίνω	peeno	to drink
πιπέρι (το)	peeperee	ground pepper
πιπεριά (η)	peeperya	pepper *(vegetable)*
πισίνα (η)	peeseena	swimming pool
πιστοποιητικό (το)	peestopyeeteeko	certificate
πιστωτική κάρτα (η)	peestoteekee karta	credit card
πίσω	peeso	behind, back
πιζάμα (η)	peezama	pyjamas
πιτσαρία (η)	peetsareea	pizzeria
πλαζ (η)	plaz	beach
πλάι	plaee	next to
πλατεία (η)	plateea	square
πληροφορίες δρομολογίων	pleeroforeeyes dhromologheeon	travel information
πληρωμή (η)	pleeromee	payment
πληρώνω	pleerono	to pay

239

πλοίο (το)	pleeo	ship
πλυντήριο (το)	pleenteereeo	washing machine
ποδήλατο (το)	podheelato	bicycle
ποδήλατο της θάλασσας	podheelato tees thalasas	pedalo
πόδι (το)	podhee	foot, leg
ποδόσφαιρο (το)	podhosfero	football
ποιος/ποια/ποιο	pyos/pya/pyo	who, which
ποιότητα (η)	peeoteeta	quality
πόλη (η)	polee	town, city
πολυκατάστημα (το)	poleekatasteema	department store
πολύς/πολλή/ πολύ	polees/polee/polee	much, many
πονόδοντος (ο)	ponodhontos	toothache
πονοκέφαλος (ο)	ponokefalos	headache
πόνος (ο)	ponos	pain
πόρτα (η)	porta	door
πορτοκάλι (το)	portokalee	orange
πορτοφόλι (το)	portofolee	wallet
πόσα;	posa?	how many?
πόσο;	poso?	how much?
πόσο κάνει;	poso kanee?	how much is it?
πόσο κοστίζει;	poso kosteezee?	how much does it cost?
ποσότητα (η)	posoteeta	quantity
ποτάμι (το)	potamee	river
πότε;	pote?	when?
ποτέ	pote	never

ποτήρι (το)	poteeree	glass *(for drinking)*
ποτό (το)	poto	drink
πού;	poo?	where?
πουκάμισο (το)	pookameeso	shirt
πούλμαν (το)	poolman	coach
πουλώ	poolo	to sell
πουρμπουάρ (το)	poorbwar	tip *(to waiter, etc.)*
πούρο (το)	pooro	cigar
πρακτορείο (το)	praktoreeo	agency
πράσινος/η/ο	praseenos/ee/o	green
πρατήριο βενζίνης	prateereeo venzeenees	petrol station
πρατήριο άρτου	prateereeo artoo	baker's
πρεσβεία (η)	presveea	embassy
πριν	preen	before
πρόεδρος (ο)	proedhros	president
προϊόν (το)	proeeon	product
προκαταβολή (η)	prokatavolee	deposit
προορισμός (ο)	pro-oreesmos	destination
προπληρώνω	propleerono	to pay in advance
προσγείωση (η)	prosgheeosee	landing
προσδεθείτε	prosdhetheete	fasten safety belts
πρόσκληση (η)	proskleesee	invitation
προσοχή (η)	prosokhee	attention
πρόστιμο (το)	prosteemo	fine
πρωί (το)	proee	morning
πρωινό (το)	proeeno	breakfast
πρωτεύουσα (η)	protevoosa	capital city

πρώτος/η/ο	protos	first
πρώτες βοήθειες	protes voeethee-es	first aid
πρώτη θέση	protee thesee	first class
πρωτοχρονιά (η)	protokhronya	New Years Day
πτήση (η)	pteesee	flight
πυροσβεστική (η)	peerosvesteekee	fire brigade
πώληση (η)	poleesee	sale
πωλητής/ ήτρια(ο/η)	poleetees/eetreea	sales assistant
πώς;	pos?	how?

ρP

ρεζέρβα (η)	rezerva	spare wheel
ρεσεψιόν (η)	resepsyon	reception *(desk)*
ρέστα (τα)	resta	change *(money)*
ρεύμα (το)	revma	current, electricity
ρόδα (η)	rodha	wheel
ροδάκινο (το)	rodhakeeno	peach
Ρόδος (η)	rodhos	Rhodes *(island)*
ρολόι (το)	roloee	watch, clock
ρούχα (τα)	rookha	clothes

σςΣ

Σαββατοκύριακο (το)	savatokeeryako	weekend
σακάκι (το)	sakakee	jacket *(menswear)*
σαμπουάν (το)	sambooan	shampoo

σάντουιτς (το)	sandweets	sandwich
σαπούνι (το)	sapoonee	soap
σβήνω	sveeno	to extinguish, to rub out
σέρβις (το)	servees	service *(of car, etc.)*
σεφ (ο)	sef	chef
σήμα (το)	seema	sign, signal
σήμερα	seemera	today
σιγά	seegha	slowly
σιδηρόδρομος (ο)	seedheerodhromos	railway
σιδηροδρομικός σταθμός	seedheerodhromeekos stathmos	railway station
σιδηροδρομικώς	seedheerodhromeekos	by rail
σινεμά (το)	seenema	cinema
σκάλα (η)	skala	ladder, staircase
σκηνή (η)	skeenee	tent, stage
σκι (το)	skee	ski
θαλάσσιο σκι	thalaseeo skee	water-skiing
σκόρδο (ο)	skordho	garlic
σκουπίδια (τα)	skoopeedhya	rubbish, refuse
σκυλί (το)	skeelee	dog
Σκοτία (η)	skoteea	Scotland
σκοτσέζικος/η/ο (η)	skotsezeekos/ee/o	Scottish *(thing)*
Σκοτσέζος/ Σκοτσέζα (ο/η)	skotsezos/skotseza	Scotsman/ Scotswoman
σόμπα (η)	soba	stove, heater
σούπα (η)	soopa	soup

σπανακόπιτα (η)	spanakopeeta	spinach pie
σπίρτο (το)	speerto	match
σπίτι (το)	speetee	house, home
σπιτικός/ή/ο	speeteekos/ee/o	homemade
σπορ (τα)	spor	sports
Σποράδες (οι)	sporadhes	the Sporades
στάδιο (το)	stadheeo	stadium, stage
σταθμεύω	stathmevo	to park
χώρος σταθμεύσεως	khoros stathmevseos	parking area
σταθμός (ο)	stathmos	station
σιδηροδρομικός σταθμός	seedheerodhro-meekos stathmos	railway station
σταθμόςυπεραστ-ικών λεωφορείων	stathmos eepera-steekon leoforeeon	bus station *(intercity)*
σταμάτα!	stamata!	stop!
στάση (η)	stasee	stop
στάση λεωφορείου	stasee leoforeeoo	bus stop
σταυροδρόμι (το)	stavrodhromee	crossroads
σταφύλι (το)	stafeelee	grape
στεγνοκαθα-ριστήριο (το)	steghnokathare-steereeo	dry-cleaner's
στιγμή (η)	steeghmee	moment
συγγνώμη	seeghnomee	sorry, excuse me
συγχαρητήρια	seengkhareeteereea	congratulations
συγχωρείτε: με...	me seengkhoreete	excuse me
σύζυγος (ο/η)	seezeeghos	husband/wife

συμπεριλαμβάνω	seempereelamvano	to include
συμπληρώνω	seempleerono	to fill in
σύμπτωμα (το)	seemptoma	symptom
συνάλλαγμα (το)	seenalaghma	foreign exchange
η τιμή του συναλλάγματος	ee teemee too seenalaghmatos	exchange rate
συνάντηση (η)	seenandeesee	meeting
συναντώ	seenando	to meet
συναυλία (η)	seenavleea	concert
συνεργείο (το)	seenergheeo	workshop, garage for car repairs
σύνορα (τα)	seenora	border, frontier
συνταγή (η)	seendaghee	prescription, recipe
συστημένη επιστολή (η)	seesteemenee epeestolee	recorded delivery
συχνά	seekhna	often
σχολείο (το)	skholeeo	school (primary)
σώμα (το)	soma	body
σωσίβιο (το)	soseeveeo	life jacket

τΤ

ταβέρνα (η)	taverna	tavern with traditional food and wine
ταινία (η)	teneea	film, strip, tape
ταμίας (ο/η)	tameeas	cashier
ταξί (το)	taksee	taxi
αγοραίο ταξί	aghoreo taksee	minicab (no meter)
ράδιο ταξί	radheeo taksee	radio taxi

ταξίδι (το)	takseedhee	journey, tour
καλό ταξίδι	kalo takseedhee	have a good trip
οργανωμένα ταξίδια	orghanomena takseedeea	organised tours
ταξιδιωτικό γραφείο	takseedheeoteeko ghrafeeo	travel agent
ταυτότητα (η)	taftoteeta	identity, identity card
ταχυδρομείο (το)	takheedhromeeo	post office
Ελληνικά Ταχυδρομεία (ΕΛΤΑ)	eleeneeka takheedhromeea	Greek Post Office
ταχύτητα/ταχύτης (η)	takheeteeta/ takheetees	speed
τελευταίος/α/ο	telefteos	last
τέλος (το)	telos	end, tax, duty
οδικά τέλη	odheeka telee	road tax
τέρμα (το)	terma	terminus, end of route
τέχνη (η)	tekhnee	art
λαϊκή τέχνη	laeekee tekhnee	folk art
τζάμι (το)	dzamee	glass *(of window)*
τζατζίκι (το)	tzatzeekee	tsatsiki *(yoghurt, cucumber and garlic)*
τηλεκάρτα (η)	teelekarta	phonecard
τηλεόραση (η)	teeleorasee	television
τηλεφώνημα (το)	teelefoneema	telephone call
τηλεφωνικός θάλαμος	teelefoneekos thalamos	phone box
τηλεφωνικός κατάλογος	teelefoneekos kataloghos	telephone directory

τηλεφωνικός κωδικός	teelefoneekos kodheekos	dialling code, area code
τι;	tee?	what?
τι είναι;	tee eenee?	what is it?
τιμή (η)	teemee	price, honour
τιμή εισιτηρίου	teemee eeseeteereeoo	price of ticket, fare
τιμοκατάλογος (ο)	teemokataloghos	price list
τιμόνι (το)	teemonee	steering wheel
τίποτα	teepota	nothing
τμήμα (το)	tmeema	department, police station
το (with neuter nouns)	to	it, the
τόκος (ο)	tokos	interest *(bank)*
τοστ (το)	tost	toasted sandwich
τουρισμός (ο)	tooreesmos	tourism
τουρίστας/στρια (ο/η)	tooreestas/streea	tourist
τουριστικός/ή/ό	tooreesteekos/ee/o	touristic
τουριστικά είδη	tooreesteeka eedhee	souvenirs
τουριστική αστυνομία	tooreesteekee asteenomeea	Tourist Police
Τουρκία (η)	toorkeea	Turkey
τραγούδι (το)	traghoodhee	song
τραγωδία (η)	traghodheea	tragedy
τράπεζα (η)	trapeza	bank
τραπεζαρία (η)	trapezareea	dining room
τραπέζι (το)	trapezee	table

τρένο (το)	treno	train
τροχαία (η)	trokhea	traffic police
τροχόσπιτο (το)	trokhospeeto	caravan, mobile home
τρώγω/τρώω	trogho/troo	to eat
τσάι (το)	tsaee	tea
τσάντα (η)	tsanda	bag
τσιγάρο (το)	tseegharo	cigarette
τυρί (το)	teeree	cheese
τυρόπιτα (η)	teeropeeta	cheese pie
τυφλός/ή/ό	teeflos/ee/o	blind
τώρα	tora	now

υΥ

υγεία (η)	eeyeea	health
στην υγειά σας	steen eeyeea sas	your health, cheers
υπηρεσία (η)	eepeereseea	service
ποσοστό υπηρεσίας	pososto eepeereseeas	service charge
υπόγειος/α/ο	eepoyeeos/a/o	underground
υπόγεια διάβαση πεζών	eepoyeea dheeavasee pezon	pedestrian subway
υπόγειος σιδηρόδρομος	eepoyeeos see-dheerodhromos	underground *(railway)*
υπολογιστής (ο)	eepologheestees	computer
υψηλός/ή/ό	eepseelos/ee/o	high
υψηλή τάση	eepseelee tasee	high voltage
ύψος (το)	eepsos	height

| ύψος περιορισμένο | eepsos pereeoreesmeno | height limit |

φΦ

φαγητό (το)	fayeeto	food, meal
φαΐ (το)	faee	food
φακός (ο)	fakos	lens, torch
φακοί επαφής	fakee epafees	contact lenses
φακές (οι)	fakes	lentils
φανάρι (το)	fanaree	traffic light, lantern
φαρμακείο (το)	farmakeeo	chemist's
φάρμακο (το)	farmako	medicine
φάω	fao	to eat
φεριμπότ (το)	fereebot	ferry boat
φέτα (η)	feta	feta cheese, slice
φιλενάδα (η)	feelenadha	girlfriend
φιλμ (το)	feelm	film
εμφανίσεις φιλμ	emfaneesees feelm	film developing
φίλος/η (ο/η)	feelos/ee	friend
φίλτρο (το)	feeltro	filter
φίλτρο λαδιού	feeltro ladheeoo	oil filter
καφές φίλτρου	kafes feeltroo	filter coffee
φλας (το)	flas	flash (camera), indicators (on car)
φοιτητής/ φοιτήτρια (ο/η)	feeteetees/ feeteetreea	student
φοιτητικό εισιτήριο (το)	feeteeteeko eeseeteereeo	student fare

φόρεμα (το)	forema	dress
φόρος (ο)	foros	tax
φούρνος (ο)	foornos	oven, bakery
ΦΠΑ (ο)	feepeea	VAT
φρένο (το)	freno	brake *(in car)*
φρέσκος/ια/ο	freskos/ya/o	fresh
φρούτο (το)	frooto	fruit
φύλακας (ο)	feelakas	guard
φύλαξη αποσκευών (η)	feelaksee aposkevon	left-luggage office
φως (το)	fos	light
φωτιά (η)	fotya	fire
φωτογραφία (η)	fotoghrafeea	photograph
φωτογραφίζω	fotoghrafeezo	to take photographs
μη φωτογρα-φίζετε	me fotoghrafeezete	no photographs
φωτογραφική μηχανή (η)	fotoghrafeekee meekhanee	camera
φωτοτυπία (η)	fototeepeea	photocopy

χΧ

χαίρετε	kherete	hello *(polite)*
χάπι (το)	khapee	pill
χάρτης (ο)	khartees	map
οδικός χάρτης	odheekos khartees	road map
χαρτί (το)	khartee	paper
χαρτί κουζίνας	khartee koozeenas	kitchen paper

χαρτομάντηλο (το)	khartomandeelo	tissue
χαρτονόμισμα (το)	khartonomeesma	banknote
χειροποίητος/η/ο	kheeropee-eetos/ee/o	handmade
χειροτεχνία (η)	kheerotekhneea	handicraft
χειρούργος (ο)	kheeroorghos	surgeon
χέρι (το)	kheree	hand, arm
χιλιόμετρο (το)	kheelyometro	kilometre
χιόνι (το)	khyonee	snow
χορός (ο)	khoros	dance
χορτοφάγος (ο/η)	khortofaghos	vegetarian
χρειάζομαι	khreeazome	to need
χρήματα (τα)	khreemata	money
χρηματοκιβώτιο (το)	khreematokeevo-teeo	safe *(for valuables)*
χρήση (η)	khreesee	use
οδηγίες χρήσεως	odheeghees khreeseos	instructions for use
χρήσιμος/η/ο	khreeseemos/ee/o	useful
χρησιμοποιώ	khreeseemopeeo	to use
χριστιανός/ή	khreesteeanos/ee	Christian
Χριστούγεννα (τα)	khreestooyena	Christmas
Καλά Χριστούγεννα	kala khreestooyena	Merry Christmas
χρόνος (ο)	khronos	time, year
χρυσός/ή/ό	khreesos/ee/o	*(made of)* gold
χρώμα (το)	khroma	colour, paint

χτες	khtes	yesterday
χυμός (ο)	kheemos	juice
χώρα (η)	khora	country
χωριάτικο ψωμί (το)	khoryateeko psomee	bread (round, flat loaf)
χωριό (το)	khoreeo	village
χωρίς	khorees	without
χώρος (ο)	khoros	area, site
αρχαιολογικός χώρος	arkheologheekos khoros	archaeological site
ιδιωτικός χώρος	eedheeoteekos khoros	private land
χώρος σταθμεύσεως	khoros stathmefseos	parking area

ψΨ

ψάρεμα (το)	psarema	fishing
ψαρεύω	psarevo	to fish
ψάρι (το)	psaree	fish
ψαρόβαρκα (η)	psarovarka	fishing boat
ψαροταβέρνα (η)	psarotaverna	fish tavern
ψητός/ή/ό	pseetos/ee/o	roasted, grilled
ψυγείο (το)	pseegheeo	fridge, radiator (of car)
ψωμί (το)	psomee	bread

ωΩ

ωτοστόπ (το)	otostop	hitchhiking
ώρα (η)	ora	time, hour
ώρες επισκέψεως	ores epeeskepseos	visiting hours
ώρες λειτουργίας	ores leetoorgheeas	opening hours
της ώρας	tees oras	freshly cooked (food)
ωραίος/α/ο	oreos/a/o	beautiful, nice
ωράριο (το)	orareeo	timetable
ως	os	as, while